❋ ❙ ❋ ❙ ❋ ❙ ❋ ❙ ❋ ❙ ❋ ❙ ❋ ❙ ❋

DEEP MACHINE LEARNING

LEARNING

A Comprehensive Beginner Developer
Guide to Deep Machine Learning
Algorithms, Concepts and Techniques

❋ ❙ ❋ ❙ ❋ ❙ ❋ ❙ ❋ ❙ ❋ ❙ ❋ ❙ ❋ ❙ ❋ ❙ ❋ ❙ ❋ ❙ ❋ ❙ ❋

Joe Grant

Table of Contents

❀ ❀ ❀ ❀ ❀ ❀ ❀ ❀ ❀ ❀ ❀ ❀ ❀ ❀ ❀ ❀

Introduction

❋ ❋ ❋ ❋ ❋ ❋ ❋ ❋ ❋ ❋ ❋ ❋ ❋ ❋ ❋ ❋ ❋ ❋

B efore we start, I want to tell you a few things about this book. It is not an easy book meant to be read in a single sitting. I've front-loaded you with math, because to understand machine learning, you'll need it. After the first few chapters, the math slowly dies down and you can immerse yourself in more text.

For this book, we'll be assuming a familiarity with mathematics and at least rudimentary knowledge of Haskell and Python. With that being said, let us begin.

Machine learning as the field of artificial intelligence is a set of paradigms, algorithms, theoretical results and applications from different fields of artificial intelligence and evolutionary models (in terms of Search) and other areas: statistics and Probabilistic (Bayesian class, distribution and tests) and other fields in mathematics and computation (there must be an awareness of the complexity of the problems and limits as well), the theory of (adaptive) control, information theory, psychology and neurobiology (neural network), and other sciences. The goal is to create programs that would be able to learn. Why should computers and machines be able to learn at all? In addition to the possibility of researching and testing different models of learning in humans and animals in psychology, there are far more practical reasons for this.

Some problems cannot simply be defined, like during practical work or if the environment in the system used is not known during its design. Let's take for example voice recognition or problems of vision in which it is necessary to customize the knowledge base about the specific voice or face detection which can be quite difficult for optimal operation.

With a large amount of data hiding nonobvious entities and relations between them and the problem can be quite hard to find. After all, think about the amount of data a program needs to go through before figuring out which, out of 7 billion, faces is yours?

Chapter 1

The First Steps

❋ ❋ ❋ ❋ ❋ ❋ ❋ ❋ ❋ ❋ ❋ ❋ ❋ ❋ ❋ ❋ ❋

In this chapter, we'll be going over the fundamentals of machine learning, going over what the initial steps you need to take are to understand it, as well as some rudimentary mathematical formulae you will need in the future.

There are methods of machine learning that are successfully applied in many areas very often. The entire field of robotics these days relies on machine learning. This is because it's extremely efficient and easy to use.

There are a few things that are quite difficult in this area, the most important one being:

Detecting knowledge (Data Mining):

Data mining is a part of machine learning which is dedicated to getting knowledge. What this means is that it's focused almost entirely on the process of getting data, rather than learning itself.

Often the amount of data and relationships in them is so great that people are virtually unable to comprehend, use, or record the knowledge as a whole. This is where machine learning and data mining come in. In these cases it is more practical, if possible, to gradually encompass such knowledge through the usage of data mining.

Machines and programs that adapt to the environment that is changing over time (dynamic systems) are common and necessary requirements in many areas. For many tasks, the aim is to find a solution which is flexible and adjusts naturally instead of using methods of artificial intelligence for which re-engineering is required after every substantial change.

Data mining enables us to know, in advance, what the program will need to learn. This lets the programmers handle it much easier.

Most of today's practically successful systems of machine learning belong to those which are "tabula rasa" as far as some knowledge is concerned (the knowledge that the student has before starting to learn). What this means is that there is no knowledge within the program before it starts learning. This is fine quite often, as usually, you'll be able to feed the program data quickly, however, sometimes it can make you run into issues.

Even though there have been many approaches attempted that aren't like this, only some methods show potential in this regard (learning explanations and Bayesian networks.) Despite this, building such methods is necessary to further advance machine learning for the advancement of, well, mankind itself.

The future of machine learning is also in systems that do not only concern one task or type of task but are also general and long-term systems (lifelong learning: independent aging agents improving performance, learning new creations, etc.) as well as in development environments (and perhaps the expansion of programming languages) that contain the necessary mechanisms needed for machine learning.

So, what does this mean? Well, current machine learning programs are specialized; for example, you'll have a chess program, and maybe it's able to beat Kasparov. On the other hand, that same program won't know what lunch is, nor how to make it.

The goal of generalist machine learning is to make programs that are smarter than people in more than one task, and eventually, just smarter in general. Granted, this is easier said than done, but it is something that the whole industry is moving towards.

In the end, it is just a matter of studying the possibility of learning a natural language as a source of experience. The bulk of today's semi-structured content of the Internet is in the form of some kind of text.

The concept of machine learning

A more precise definition of the concept of machine learning would be:

Definition 1.1: A Program (machine) M learns from experience E in relation to the class of tasks T and performance measurement P (rate is de f Nisan of the trait or set of traits that will have to be defined), if the performance measures P program improves related tasks T after the experience of E.

In the case of recognition of written text T is recognizing and class forging words or letters in the figure, P is the percentage of correctly recognized, E is a set of training which forms the base of the given images of letters and words and their class. A classic example is the Seymour program that teaches to play ladies. The performance measure is then the ability to win an opponent after the experience gained in playing against himself or the opponents who can play. The object of learning can be different conceptions of the world, that is, the computable structure:

Many functions may be broadly task searched if the map of some papers where the mapping hypothesis h (the same arity) and the set of training detachment S is a number of pairs of the set values.

The goal is for h from a class of functions H that is better, to coincide with f (h = f, ideally). For example, the evaluation function in game theory, which is usually represented by a parameter vector (for example, the LMS rule learning) logic programs, frames are the basic form of conceptualization of the world in which the solution of a problem is sought is the language of PR1 or one of its "dialects" (e.g. PROLOG) and other formalizations.

Types of learning and basic characteristics

The basis of the division of learning types is related to the learning of functions, but it is perceived similarly to other learning objects:

Supervised when the setpoint function in the set of training (trivial example can be interpolation or plotting a curve.) This means that you've told the program where to begin with the learning.

Unsupervised when the value of the set is not set in the set of training features (usually reduced to a problem of class forging i.e. Such that the value of the previous case of a class belongs to the set.) In this case, you haven't told the program starts learning, and it figures it out itself.

Hypothesis as the scientific significance of the conceptualization of the world (environment) and its accuracy as the starting measure of performance are common to most of the systems of machine learning. The structure of a prototype of such a classical system (e.g. Many problems games, classes of neural networks, different systems of pattern recognition or class f cation, etc.) Is shown with four related areas:

Let's see, for example, a program that checks, with the evaluation function, how to have a coefficient whose f, w and x values of the condition table in n many b domains and functions as the object of instruction. The performance system and the working hypothesis V give some sort of solution (the solution trace, e.g., the move sheet, i.e., the state b and the estimate of their values) taken by the critic, there is a set of training made by couples (b; V o (b)), but these critics associate, experience "created after each batch by calling for a given variable in the party (especially for which there is no value in the set of training) takes the assessment value in the (b) a V (succ (b)) (the rule of evaluation of the value of the training, where succ (b) is the status of the board after the program moves, i.e. the one in which the next opponent's action is expected). This is particularly useful if the only experience available resulting in games played against itself (this is additionally useful for systems that cannot overcome the problem j, bad experience "when they learn of an opponent who does not know well to play Samuel's example). Safely it is known only that someone gained or lost the game, and in this way, the program assesses what happened. Between the two values of the function evaluations, the program will find bits of knowledge to learn. It turns out that this is a very late methods of learning in special cases (learning with reinforcement). It can be shown that it necessarily strives for the best solution (e.g. perceptron, in cases where such a solution exists). The generalizer is a component that has the role of applying acquired knowledge based on learning rules and its result is a new hypothesis e.g. LMS (Least Mean Squares) implies that the best hypothesis minimizes the sum of the squares of errors (the differences of some values from the set of training and hypotheses) $E = P (b; V o (b)) 2 S [V o (b) \textrm{¡} V (b)] 2$, and this is realized, for example, by the following iterative rule of learning:

$$w i w w i + ' [V o (b) ¡ V (b)] x i$$

Where ' 2 (0 ; 1) parameter of learning speed. The new hypothesis should give each of these cycles (epochs) a better performance. On the basis of it, the current training set and the learning strategy creates a new experimental generator (a blank board in the specific case). In the general case, many variations of this type of learning are possible, where in addition to the different choice of experience and the generation of cases, a different learning strategy can be chosen, which also implies a different function of evaluation (which is sometimes the object of learning, objective function) and its representation, as well as a different learning algorithm (e.g. gradient method, dynamic programming, etc.) Generalization. It asks many questions about how to implement the described components optimally, what kind of training is needed (how many pairs, how diversity affects the ability to generalize the learned material.

How (and why) limit the class of available hypotheses and others can be a bit harder to determine. In addition, it is very important to correctly select the members of a set of training and performance evaluation modes. These modes of learning will take pairs of exercises to achieve the optimal time and learning performance? If a set of training pairs is also the only source of knowledge for the learning system, and the only source for learning performance assessments is to make sure that the system will later work successfully with unknown pairs outside of training, how much is generalized? A common practical method for achieving this is the division of the n training exercises by n partitions (n folds, where n is usually from 0 to 3 and 10), wherein n iterations are taken to ensure one partition is used to evaluate performance and others for learning. For some other methods, more details will be in the next chapters. The aim of the further text is, first of all, to overview the different learning methods without special consideration of details except as an illustration of how to apply and review the content.

Neural Networks And Genetic Algorithms

Neural networks and genetic algorithms (evolution programming) are the paradigms of Soft Computing and the areas naturally support many aspects of machine learning. Let's take a look at some other things. NA feedback systems a good example of a system in which machine learning can be applied. If you are under then class NA with feedback propagation (and some others). With generalized prototype systems of machine learning you can recognize all its elements are tasks that the system must do, system performance, which is measured (for example, numerical accuracy NM or efficiency class f), as well as experience and sets of training.

The strategy of training and structure can be very different from the described case and the prototype. This is a case which is usually a result of a specific outcome of combining fresh surface domains and problems that are solved by such systems. NM show the characteristics of inductive systems of machine learning have the ability of generalization based on the given examples.

Genetic algorithms, in general, can be seen as machine learning algorithms to learn (or to find) the hypothesis where the hypothesis space is conditioned specifically to it. With its task rises the question: what role has experience played in it? The objective function can be set or changed examples, and then we have the experience and learning. For example, it, which generates a program (or other computable formalism) experienced the given characteristics. Then some metrics such as accuracy results on the basis of the given input (instances), length of the BDA or efficiency define the objective function.

Chapter 2

Back To The Basics With Python

❀ ❁ ❀ ❁ ❀ ❁ ❀ ❁ ❀ ❁ ❀ ❁ ❀ ❁ ❀ ❁ ❀ ❁ ❀ ❁ ❀

In this chapter, we'll be looking at simple tests that you can do with classification using the Python programming language.

Have you been using the classification as a type of machine learning? Probably yes, even if you did not know about it. Example: The email system has the ability to automatically detect spam. This means that the system will analyze all incoming messages and mark them as spam or non-spam.

Often, you, as an end user, have the option to manually tag messages as spam, to improve the ability to detect spam. This is a form of machine learning where the system takes the examples of two types of messages: spam and so-called ham (the typical term for "non-spam email") and using these cases automatically classify incoming mails fetched.

What is a classification? Using the examples from the same domain of the problem belonging to the different classes of the model train or the "generate rules" which can be applied to a (previously unknown) examples.

Dataset Iris is a classic collection of data from the 1930s; This is one of the first examples of modern statistical classifications. The data set is a collection of several morphological measurements of iris flowers. These measurements allow us to identify the different types of flower.

Today, the species are identified through DNA, but in the 30s the role of DNA in genetics had not yet been recorded. Four characteristics were selected for each plant sepal length (length of cup slip) sepal width (width of cup slip) petal length, and petal width. There are three classes that identify the plant: Iris setosa, Iris versicolor, and Iris virginica.

Formulation of the problem

This dataset has four characteristics. In addition, each plant species was recorded, as well as the value of class characteristics. The problem we want to solve is: Given these examples, can we anticipate a new type of flower in the field based on measurements?

This is the problem of classification or supervised learning, where based on the selected data, we can "generate rules" that can later be applied to other cases. Examples for readers who do not study botany are: filtering unwanted email, intrusion detection in computer systems and networks, detection of fraud with credit cards, etc.

Data Visualization will present a kind of triangle, circle type, and virginica type of mark x.

First, read the data.

```
from matplotlib import pythonplotting as plt
import numpy as np from sklearn.datasets
import load_iris # read from the data using load_iris sklearn
load_iris data = ()
 # load_iris returns an object that contains the value of
features
features class = data.data feature_names =
data.feature_names target = data.target target_names =
data.target_names
figs = plt.subplots axes (2, 3) according to # visualizing three
pairs of the two lines = [(0, 1), (0, 2), (0, 3), (1, 2), (1, 3 ), (2, 3)]
# pairing characteristics color_markers = [( 'r', '>'), ( 'g', 'o'), ( 'b',
'x'), ] # Setting of the colors and markers
for and, (po, p1), and enumerate (pairs): ax = axes.flat [i] for t
in range (3): c, = color_markers marker [t]
# uses a different pair of colors / a marker for each class
ax.scatter (features [target == t, po], features [target == t p1]
marker = marker, c = c) ax.set_xlabel (feature_names [po])
ax.set_ylabel (feature_names [p1]) ax.set_xticks ([])
ax.set_yticks ([]) fig.tight_layout () fig.savefig ( 'figurure1.png')
```

A simple classification model. The objective, as stated above, is to separate the three types of flowers.

What do we do next? We seek boundary separation.

```
# NumPy will use to create an array of strings: >>> labels =
target_names [target] # Petal characteristic length is at
position 2
>>> plength = features [:, 2] >>> is_setosa = (labels == 'setosa')
# This step is essential
 >>> max_setosa = plength [is_setosa] .max () >>>
min_non_setosa plength = [~ is_setosa], min () >>> print (
'Maximum setosa of: {0}.'. format (max_setosa)) Maximum of
setosa: 1.9. >>> print ( 'Minimum of others: {0}.'. Format
(min_non_setosa))
Minimum of others: 3.0.  13 simple classification model.
```

With this we made a simple model: if the length of the petals is less than 2, then this flower is Iris setosa; otherwise, the plants are Iris virginica or Iris versicolor. This is our first classification model that separates the very good flowers Iris setosa from the other two species (with no errors). However, in this case, we are not actually engaged in machine learning. Instead, we looked at data itself, seeking the separation between the classes. We can use machine learning when we write the code that automatically searches for this separation.

Separation With The Smallest Error.

The problem of separation Iris setosa compared to the other two species was very easy. However, we can immediately see what is the best threshold for distinguishing Iris virginica from the Iris versicolor.

We can even see that we will never achieve perfect separation with these characteristics. We can, however, look for the best possible separation or separation that makes the slightest mistake.

First, we select a set of instances that do not belong to the class.

```
>>> features include = [~ is_setosa] # ~ a boolean negation
operator >>> = labels labels [~ is_setosa] >>> is_virginica =
(labels == 'virginica') # creates a new target variable,
is_virginica
```

Thereafter in the loop pass all possible characteristics and thresholds to determine which will result in better accuracy.

Accuracy is roughly defined as the ratio of the case (instances) which model has been correctly classified and the total number of examples.

```
# Set value evening accuracy to the lowest possible value
best_acc = -1.0
# Go through loop through all the characteristics and range for
fi
(features.shape [1]): # Test all possible threshold values for
feature fi features
thresh = [: fi] .copy () thresh.sort () and for t thresh
# take a feature vector fi = feature_i features [:, fi]
```

```
# generate a prediction using t as the threshold before =
(feature_i> t)
# accuracy of the ratio of correct predictions acc = (front ==
is_virginica) .mean () 17 separation with the smallest error.
# Will test whether a comparison of the "greater" or "less" than
the threshold provides a better result
rev_acc = (front == ~ is_virginica) .mean () if rev_acc> acc:
reverse = True = acc rev_acc else: reverse = False # If the
accuracy greater than previous, remember memorial
threshold.
 if acc> best_acc: best_acc acc best_fi = = = best_t fi t
best_reverse = reverse
```

Variable best_fi, best_t and best_reverse make our model. This information is necessary to classify new, unknown objects, that is, we have assigned the value of the class characteristics as follows:

```
def is_virginica_test (fi, t, reverse, example): "Apply threshold
model to a new example"
test = example [fi]> t if reverse: test = test not return test
```

How does this model work? If you start at the overall data model which has been identified as the best decision based on the width of the petals. One way to gain insight into the functioning of the model is a visualization of the border decision.

In the past pages, we've seen that the screen displays two regions: white and gray (shaded). Any item that belongs to the white region will be classified as Iris virginica, while each point of the corresponding shaded side to be classified as Iris versicolor.

Code that draws the model can be found in the source code, under file 2.

The model has already discussed a simple model that achieves 94% accuracy on the entire data set. However, this estimate may be too optimistic: the data we use to define what would be the threshold was then used to estimate the model.

What I really want to do is to assess the ability of generalization model. In other words, we should measure the performance of the algorithm in cases where classified information, which is not trained, is used.

Transmitting device stringent evaluation and use the "delayed" (Casually, Held-out) data is one way to do this. The information will be separated by making a portion of the data used to train the model, and the second part to be tested or assessed

```
file cho2 / heldout.py.
import numpy as np from sklearn.
datasets from import load_iris threshold import fit_model,
accuracy data = load_iris ()
include = data [ 'data'] labels = data [ 'target_names'] [data [a'
target ']] # We remove setosa examples
: is_setosa = (labels ==' setosa ') features include = [~ is_setosa]
= labels labels [~ is_setosa]
```

```
Classify # - virginica or Versicolor is_virginica = (labels =='
virginica ') 23 Rate model. # Share information on training and
test data testing np.tile = ([True, False], 50) # testing = [True,
False, True, False, True, False ...]
training = ~ # testing training set contains what which is not in
the test set of model = fit_model (features [training]
is_virginica [training]) train_accuracy = accuracy (features
[training] is_virginica [training], model) test_accuracy =
accuracy (features [testing], is_virginica [testing], model ) print
( ' " \ Training accuracy was {0: 1%}. Testing was accuracy {1}
1% (N = {2}). "
Format (train_accuracy, test_accuracy, testing.sum ()))
```

What do you get if you run the previous code? Training accuracy
was 96.0%. Testing accuracy was 90.0% (N = 50). What actually
happened? Accuracy in case of the just trained set of data (which is
a subset of the data) is obviously higher than before.

However, the accuracy of the test data is lower! While this may
surprise an inexperienced person who is engaged in machine
learning, it's expected to be lower by veterans. Generally, the
accuracy of testing is lower than the accuracy of training. Using the
previous examples you should be able to plot a graph of this data.
The graph will show the boundary decisions.

Consider what would happen if the decision to limit some of the
cases near the border were not there during the training? It is easy
to conclude that the boundaries move slightly to the right or left.

NOTES: In this case, the difference between the accuracy of the measured data for training and testing is not great. When using a complex model, it is possible to get 100% accuracy in training and very low accuracy testing! In other words, the accuracy of the training set is a too optimistic assessment of how good your algorithm is. Experiments always measured and reported the accuracy of testing and accuracy on the set of examples that are not being used for the training!

A possible problem with the hold-out validation is that we are only using half of the data used for training. However, if you use too much data for training, assessment error testing is done on a very small number of examples. Ideally, we would use all the data for the training and all the data for testing, but it was impossible.

A good approximation of the impossible ideals is a method called cross-validation. The simplest form of cross-validation is Leave-one-out cross-validation. From the training data we will be excluding one example; this trains the model and checks whether it has properly classified the excluded example.

This process is then repeated for all elements in the data set.

```
>>>
>>> correct = 0.0 for ei in range (len (features)) # I select all
examples of the position `ei`
: training np.ones = (len (features) bool) training [ei] = False
testing model training
```

```
~ = fit_model (features [training] is_virginica [training]) =
predictions predict (model, features [testing]) correct np.sum +
= (== predictions is_virginica [testing ]) = acc >>> correct / float
(len (features)) >>> print ( "Accuracy: {o: 1%}. 'format (acc))
Accuracy: 87.0%
```

When using cross-checking, each example was tested on a model trained without taking into account that data. Therefore, cross-validation is a reliable estimate of the possibilities of generalization model. The main problem with the previous method of validation is a need for training of a large number (the number grows to the size of the set).

Instead, let's look at the so-called v-fold validation. If, for example, using 5-fold cross-validation, the data is divided into five parts, of which in each iteration 4 parts are used for training and one for testing.

The number of parts in the initial set of components depends on the size of the event, the time required for the training model, and so on. When generating fold data, it is very important to be balanced.

What are false negative and false positive results?

An example in the field of medicine: False negative - the result of a test is negative, but it is not actually true. This can cause the patient not receiving treatment for a serious illness.

A false-positive - result of the test is positive when the patient, in fact, does not have the disease; This may lead to additional tests for the confirmation or unacceptable treatment, which may still have consequences, including the adverse effects of the treatment. In practice, sometimes has to be a compromise between the frequency of false positive and false negative results.

What are examples of false positive and false negative results for filtering unwanted email, systems detecting intrusions into computer networks, and systems for detecting credit card fraud?

Ka complex classifiers

The model that classifies on the basis of the value of threshold characteristics is simple. There are a number of more complex models. How to choose the right one? It is necessary to pay attention to the structure of the model, how to model decision-making, the procedure time, how do we determine the parameters of the model, function loss or gain, optimizing a model in such a way to make fewer mistakes type of false positive or false-negative results.

We will analyze one dataset from agriculture, seeds - which is still small, but still too high for the visualization of data (i.e. drawing that we have done with IRIS). The data set consists of measurements of wheat seed. A data packet contains seven continuous features which do not include the non-existent values: A area, perimeter P, compactness $C = 4\pi A / P^2$, the length of the core, the width of the core, asymmetry coefficient and the length of the core grooves.

The seeds dataset and nearest neighbor data set both follow the same rules. There are three classes that correspond to the varieties of wheat: Canadian, Coma, and Rosa. As before, the goal is to classify species based on these morphological measurements.

Unlike the dataset iris flower, which was collected in the 1930s, this is a newer set of data and its characteristics are automatically calculated from digital images. Note: The University of California at Irvine (UCI) held an on-line repository of datasets for machine learning. Both sets (iris and seeds) used in these exercises were taken there.

The repository is available at: http://archive.ics.uci.edu/ml/

Let's proceed to take a closer look at the features, you'll notice that the compactness is not an independent feature, but a function of surface area and perimeter. In practice, it is often useful to generate new combined characteristics. Attempts to create new features are referred to as engineered features (also Feature engineering).

This activity will affect the performance of the classifier: a simple algorithm to achieve better performance in a well-defined field of characteristics or the not-so well-defined characteristics.

To invoke good characteristics, it is necessary to know the specific problem to solve. In other words, even before you start collecting data you need to know what information we collect is worth, and how to pick apart the parts that are less useful or useless.

Fortunately, for a large number of problem domains, there is enough literature which describes the characteristics and types of features suitable for solving the problem. It is natural to ask whether we can automatically select good features. This problem is known as a selection of features (also Feature selection).

There are many methods that have been proposed to solve this problem, but in practice, very simple ideas work best. For simple problems that are currently out there, there is no need to reject some features.

In cases where we have thousands of topics, shedding most of them can make the rest of the process much faster.

This method is also based on memory or instances. Belonging to a family of learning algorithms that, instead of performing explicit generalizations, compares new instances with instances that are already past the training phase and are in the memory.

Learning based on instances is a kind of lazy learning. Lazy learning in artificial intelligence is a desirable feature of learning if there is a requirement for a constantly changing knowledge base, where any such change does not entail repeating the whole process of learning, but only efficient incremental additions of knowledge.

A common feature of these methods is that they all accommodate in training instance memory structures and use them for directorial classification. The simplest form of a memory structure of the multidimensional space is a defining characteristic. Each training instance is represented as a point in space.

Classification of new instances is done according to the principle of the nearest neighbors, wherein a new instance is compared with the instances from the learning set using the defined metrics. Metrics can be defined as different instances based on the value of their attributes and corresponds to an intuitive understanding of the similarities so that if they are instances of similar properties, the distance is less.

The new instance is classified based on the search for a set of learning with the aim of finding the instance that is nearest in terms of distance.

Training: Placement of training instances. Classification: The specific instance x contains k nearest neighbors among the instances in the training set. The largest number of neighbors of the same class determines the class instance. As you can see, there is no training phase into common sense. The price of this is slower decision-making procedures, because in order to classify one message we have to count the distance from the training of all messages and find k nearest neighbors.

Figure algorithm for k = 1, k = 2 and k = 3- acceptance criteria and the elimination of instances mainly represent an irreversible, greedy strategy of ML. The simplest criterion is that an instance is tested according to the result of classification using the previously isolated representative instances.

In case of incorrect classification, it is added to the collection of representative instances because it is evident that changes the class boundaries. If the correct classification of instances is then declared as redundant because the information it carries is already contained in the set with which it is classified then you're done!

Disadvantages of this criterion for the selection of instances:

- In the initial stage of the search process, there is a genuine chance of rejection of instances that can prove important for the accuracy of the resulting classification models.

- The elected representative subset of instances depends not only on the initial set, but the order of evaluation instances.

- In addition to the selection of instances of memory, the classification model can be influenced by modifying the function of distance.

Equal impact of all attributes in the instance implies that the final result is one of the properties of Euclidean distances. When it comes to practice, issues where all attributes have the same value for the classification process may arise. Modification of the Euclidean distance includes the introduction of the weights of the attribute.

If the wi mark weighting value associated with the attribute Ai, then modified Euclidean distance instances by x and y can be presented as follows: $dw\ x, y\ i = = 1\ n\ wi\ 2\ xi - yi\ 2$ This is where we apply what we've learned so far, as well as adding a bit to it. So far we have used handmade classification codes. However, due to their libraries, Python is an appropriate language for machine learning.

Library scikit-learn has become a standard library for many machine learning tasks, including classification. In the following, we use the implementation of exposure to the nearest neighbor method.

Two basic methods of scikit-learn for classification are: fit (features, labels) - this is a step that creates learning model parameters; predict (features) - this method can be called only after learning and restores prediction for one or more inputs. The implementation of our nearest neighbors begin importing the data from the sub-module facility KneighborsClassifier sklearn.neighbors: >>> import from sklearn.neighbours KNeighborsClassifier Module scikit-learn imported as sklearn (sometimes you'll discover that the scikit-learn mentions using this short name instead of full name).

All functional sklearn modules are sub-modules, such as sklearn.neighbours. Now we can create an instance of the object classifier. In the constructor we determine the number of neighbors to consider:

```
>>> classifier = KNeighborsClassifier (n_neighbors = 1) If you
do not specify the number of neighbors, it means 5, which
sometimes can be a good choice for classification.
We want to use cross-validation to look at our data  >>> from
sklearn.cross_validation import KFold >>> kf = KFold (len
(features), n_folds = 5, shuffle = True) means >>> = [] >>> for
training, testing and kf: # The first train model fit method, and
then assayed by the method predict
```

```
classifier.fit (features [training], labels [training]) = prediction
classifier.predict (features [testing]) = curmean np.mean
(prediction == labels [testing]) means.append (curmean) >>>
print ( "Mean accuracy: {: 1%}. 'format (np.mean (means)))
Mean accuracy: 90.5%
```

For this data set, with this algorithm, we obtain 90.5% accuracy. As mentioned above, cross-validation accuracy is lower than the accuracy of the training, but this is a credible performance evaluation model. We will now examine the boundary decision. To visualize this, simplify the case and analyze only two characteristics (area and compactness).

When you plot this, do you notice something strange in the chart? We can observe that the regions are split almost vertical lines and ask the question why the graph looks like it. The values on the x axis (area) are in the range from 10 to 22, while the numerical values on the y-axis are in the range from 0.75 to 1. This is derived from the measuring unit to which the value of the described features is derived from.

This means that a small change in one axis is actually much larger than the small changes on the other axis. In other words, when calculating the distance between the points, in most cases take only the x-axis.

This is also a good example of why it's a good idea to visualize our data and check whether there are any "surprises".

How can we solve the problem? It is necessary to normalize all the features. This can be solved in several ways, but one of the possible is the z-score normalization. Let f old value characteristics, f 'new value, μ mean value and standard deviation σ, where μ and σ values are estimated based on data for training. Normalization is performed in the following way: $f' = f - \mu$ σ After a z-score normalization, a value $f' = 0$ corresponding to the value $f = \mu$, a negative value ?? 'correspond to values less than the mean value μ, the positive values of f 'correspond' to values greater than the mean value μ.

How else can we solve the problem? Using the module scikit-learn normalization simply performed as a step in data preprocessing. We will use the pipeline in which the first element is normalization and the other classification. In order to do that, we import the class to work with a pipeline and scaling features as follows:

```
>>> import from sklearn.pipeline Pipeline
>>> import from sklearn.preprocessing StandardScaler Next,
do the following:
>>> classifier = KNeighborsClassifier (n_neighbors = 1)
>>> Pipeline classifier = ([( 'norm', StandardScaler ()), (knn
"classifier)])
```

Constructor pipelines require a list of pairs of the type (p, clf). Each pair corresponds to one step in the pipeline, wherein the first element is designated by the string step, while the other element is an object that performs the transformation.

After normalization, each feature is in the same units (technically, each feature is without dimension, because there is no measurement unit). If now we launch a classifier based on the nearest neighbor method, we get 93% of the accuracy of 5-fold cross-validation with the code previously discussed and you can see that both characteristics affect the outcome. In the complete data set, everything happens on the seven-dimensional space, which is difficult to visualize, but the same principle applies: Several characteristics dominated in the original data, but after normalization have all the hallmarks of the same character. Seeds dataset and nearest neighbor method.

The classifiers we used so far are binary. The classifiers we used for Seeds dataset are multiclass. A multiclass problem can be solved with a series of binary decisions.

Chapter 3

Clustering In Python

❋ ❘ ❋ ❘ ❋ ❘ ❋ ❘ ❋ ❘ ❋ ❘ ❋ ❘ ❋ ❘ ❋ ❘ ❋ ❘ ❋ ❘ ❋ ❘ ❋

What is the difference between classification and clustering? In the previous chapter, we dealt with classification as a type of supervised learning.

NOTE: In these examples, we'll be using the dataset available at: http://www.cs.columbia.edu/~blei/lda-c/ap.tgz

Training data for the models were marked, and the model was further used to classify previously unknown instances.

We ask the following question: what can we do if we do not have marked models for training the model? Obviously, the classification model cannot be built. But we can find specific templates in the data. Formally said, in the modern field of machine learning, the following approaches dominate: inductive learning, analytical learning (logic analogy), case-based learning (analogy with human memory), neural networks (analogy with neurobiology), genetic algorithms (analogy with evolution) and hybrid models (multiple access combination).

Of utmost importance for current practice in the field of computing and artificial intelligence is inductive learning. The essence of this type of learning is learning based on available examples. In everyday language, we can call it learning from experience. With regard to the object of learning, the most important is the learning of functional, that is, input-output mappings.

Key elements in the inductive learning of functional mappings are unknown mapping, training a set of input-output pairs and a set of hypotheses within which we choose the final hypothesis through a training algorithm. The inputs are, as a rule, n dimensional vectors. In most literature, they are referred to as: vectors of signs, patterns, examples and instances. The input vector components are called attributes and can be continuous (infinite number of values) and discrete (a finite number of values).

The output space can be categorized with K-values when a trained system performs classification (the output is called a tag, class, category, or decision) or realistic when the trained system realizes regression (functional estimator). There are two types of training. Training can be divided into training with loading, non-teacher training, and reinforcement learning. For training with the teacher, i.e. Supervised learning, you are monitoring the program, and making adjustments while it learns, while for unsupervised learning you leave it to its own devices.

```
{>> print (X_train.getrow (3) .toarray ()) [[o o o o 1 1 o 1 o o o o
o o o o o o o o 1 o o o]] >>> print (X_train.getrow (4) .toarray
()) [[o o o o 3 3 o 3 o o o o o o o o o o o o o 3 o o o ]].
```

> *We will change the dist_raw function to calculate the distance between normalized vectors. def dist_norm (v1, v2):*
>
> *v1_normalized = v1 / sp.linalg.norm (v1.toarray ())*
>
> *v2_normalized = v2 / sp.linalg.norm (v2.toarray ())*
>
> *delta = v1_normalized*
>
> *v2_normalized return sp.linalg. norm (delta.toarray ())*
>
> *In this case, when comparing a new sentence with all posts, a different result is obtained. From the program exit, it can be seen that now post 3 and post 4 are similarly similar to the new sentence.*
>
> *=== Post 0 with dist = 1.41: This is a toy post about machine learning. Actually, it does not contain much interesting stuff.*
>
> *=== Post 1 with dist = 0.86: Imaging databases provide storage capabilities.*
>
> *=== Post 2 with dist = 0.92: Most imaging databases save images permanently.*
>
> *=== Post 3 with dist = 0.77: Imaging databases store data.*

Imaging databases store data

The best post is 3 with dist = 0.77. If we look again at post 2, we will notice that the words "bridge", "save", "images" and "permanently" are not found in the new sentence. The impact of these words on the meaning of the post or the amount of information they carry is different. Words like "bridge" often appear in all different contexts and are called stop words. Stop words do not contain as much information and do not need to attach the same meaning to words like "images", which do not often appear in different contexts.

The best option would be to remove all the words that are so common that they do not help to differentiate between different texts.

Removing Stopwords

Since the removal of the stop is a typical step in the processing of natural languages, it is sufficient to set the stop_words parameter to a language whose stop we want to remove. For English, 318 stop words are removed, of which the first 20 are listed.

> *>>> vectorizer = CountVectorizer (min_df = 1, stop_words = 'English')*
> *>>> sorted (vectorizer.get_stop_words ()) [0:20] ['a', 'about', 'above', 'across' 'after', 'afterwards',' again ',' against ',' all ',' almost ',' alone ',' along ',' already ',' also ',' though ',' always', 'am ',' among, ',' amongst '] After removing stop words, 7 tokenized stop words from our example are removed from our example: "about", "is", "it", "most", "much", "not ",and "this".*

After removing the stop word, we get the following similarity measures (note that the distance of posts 1 and 2 of the new sentence is now the same, because they have the same number of words that they do not have in the new sentence):

> *=== Post 0 with dist = 1.41: This is a toy post about machine learning. Actually, it does not contain much.*
> *=== Post 1 with dist = 0.86: Imaging databases provide storage capabilities.*

> *=== Post 2 with dist = 0.86: Most imaging databases save*
> *images permanently.*
> *=== Post 3 with dist = 0.77: Imaging databases store data.*
> *=== Post 4 with dist = 0.77: Imaging databases store data.*
> *Imaging databases store data. Imaging databases store data.*
> *Best post is 3 with dist = 0.77*

Until now, we have seen different forms of words and words similar to different words. For example, Post 2 contains the words "imaging" and "images".

Since words point to the same or very similar concept, we can count them together. So, we need a function that will reduce the word to a form that is suitable for counting. SciKit does not have this feature yet, but you can download the free Natural Language Toolkit (NLTK) tool - this tool provides a stemmer that can be easily used with CountVectorizer. NLTK provides more stemmer - this is logical because each language has different rules for bringing words into the basic form.

For English we will use SnowballStemmer. Please note that the result of this operation does not necessarily result in the correct English words. Here's an example of how to download NLTK:

```
>>> import nltk.stem
>>> s = nltk.stem.SnowballStemmer ('english')
>>> s.stem ("graphics") u'graphic '
>>> s.stem ("imaging") u'imag '
>>> s.stem ("image") u'imag'
```

```
>>> s.stem ("imagination") u'imagin '
>>> s.stem ("imagine") u'imagin'
```

Example 2:

```
>>> s.stem ("buys") u'buy '
>>> s.stem ("buying") u'buy' Note - this operation sometimes
does not return the stem form. For example, the stench of the
word "bought" should result in the word "buy". >>> s.stem
("bought") u' bought
. Expand CountVectorizer class NLTK functionality: import
nltk.stem english_stemmer = nltk.stem.SnowballStemmer
('english')) class StemmedCountVectorizer (CountVectorizer):
def build_analyzer (self): analyzer = super
(StemmedCountVectorizer, self) .build_analyzer () return
lambda doc : (english_stemmer.stem (w) for w in analyzer
(doc)) vectorizer = StemmedCountVectorizer (min_df = 1,
stop_words = 'english')
```

What does the code do?

Previous code: converts all letters into lowercase letters in the pre-process phase, separates all of the words in the process of tokenization, draws a stop word, and converts words into stem form. After launching this code, another tag, or word form, was dropped, because after stemming, the words "images" and "imaging" are identical.

```
print (vectorizer.get_feature_names ()) [u'actual ', u'capabl',
u'contain ', u'data', u'databas ', u'imag', u'interest ', u'learn', u
'machin', u'perman ', u'post', u'provid ', u'save', u'storag ',
u'store', u'stuff ', u'toy']
```

What is the post most similar to "imaging databases"?

```
=== Post o with dist = 1.41: This is a toy post about machine
learning. Actually, it does not contain much interesting stuff.
=== Post 1 with dist = 0.86: Imaging databases provide storage
capabilities.
=== Post 2 with dist = 0.63: Most imaging databases save
images permanently.
=== Post 3 with dist = 0.77: Imaging databases store data.
=== Post 4 with dist = 0.77: Imaging databases store data.
Imaging databases store data. Imaging databases store data.
The best post is 2 with dist = 0.63
```

For now, we can say that we have found a good way to form a compact vector based on a silent text post. Let's go back a little bit to think about what the value of the tag really means. Values are derived based on the number of occurrences of appointments in the post, and our assumption is that higher value means that the term is of greater importance.

However, in this case, it can be concluded that longer documents have priority over short shifts. Therefore, it is necessary to normalize counting based on the length of the document. Also, it is necessary to remove useless terms (for example, the term "subject", which is found in almost every post).

Simple implementation of TF-IDF:

```
import scipy as sp def tfidf (term, doc, corpus): tf = doc.count
(term) / len (doc) num_docs_with_term = len ([d for d in corpus
if term in d] = sp.log (lens (corpus) / num_docs_with_term)
return tf * idf
```

For the given corpus D containing the tokenized documents a, abb and abc, the previous function returns the following:

```
>>> a, abb, abc = ["a"], ["a", "b", "b"], ["a "," b "," c "] >> D = [a,
abb, abc] >>> print (tfidf (" a ", a, D)) 0.0 >>> print (tfidf (" a "
abb, D)) 0.0 >>> print (tfidf ("a", abc, D)) 0.0 Based on this, we
conclude that the term is insignificant because it is
everywhere.
For the given corpus D containing the tokenized documents a,
abb and abc the previous function returns: >>> print (tfidf ("b",
abb, D)) 0.270310072072 >>> print (tfidf ("b", abc, D))
0.135155036036 >>> print (tfidf ("c", abc, D)) 0.366204096223
```

Based on this we conclude that the term b is more significant for the abb document than for the document abc because it appears twice in it.

SciKit implementation (we use TfidfVectorizer inherited by CountVectorizer) is given by the following code: from skleparn.feature_extraction.text import TfidfVectorizer class StemmedTfidfVectorizer (TfidfVectorizer): def build_analyzer (self): analyzer = super (TfidfVectorizer, self) .build_analyzer () return lambda doc: (english_stemmer.stem (w) for w in analyzer (doc)) vectorizer = StemmedTfidfVectorizer (min_df = 1, stop_words = 'english', decode_error = 'ignore')

There are a few drawbacks to this. Relationships between words are not taken into account. For example, the words "cars hits wall" and "wall hits car" will have the same vector character. There is also a problem with negations. For example, the words "I will eat ice cream" and "I will not eat ice cream" will have very similar vector features and if they have the opposite meaning.

This problem is solvable if only individual words are taken into account when counting words, but bigrams (word pairs) or trigrams (three words in a row). There is a problem with misspelled words. Although it is clear to the reader that the words "database" and "databas" have the same meaning, that is, a writing error, the approach we use will treat them as two different words. Naturally, you can treat them as the same, but this generally quite impractical.

However, the focus of this chapter is on clustering, not on the processing of natural languages, so we will use the approach of the bag of words for further cluster analysis.

Clustering, i.e. cluster analysis is the search for groups of objects such that objects in a group are similar (or related), and that objects in different groups are different (or disconnected). Clustering is used to view documents from the same group, group gene and protein having the same functionality, grouping actions with similar price changes, etc. For example, rainfall clustering in Australia.

There is a significant difference between the partition and the hierarchical cluster set. Partitioning clustering is the division of the data set into non-overlapping subsets (clusters) such that each data is exactly in a subset.

Hierarchical clustering is a set of nesting clusters organized in the form of a hierarchical tree. Hierarchical clustering can be traditional and non-traditional, resulting in a traditional and nontraditional dendrogram.

Cluster analysis 50 Clustering using the K-environment algorithm. K-means is an access to a clustering partition in which each cluster is associated with a centroid (center point) and each point is assigned to a cluster with the nearest centroid.

The number of clusters K must be specified. The basic algorithm is extremely simple:

1. Select K points as initial centroids.

2. Repeat.

3. From K clusters by assigning all points to the nearest centroid.

4. Recompute centroid for each cluster.

5. Repeat until the centroids do not change.

The initial centroid is often chosen in a random way. The resulting clusters may vary in successive program execution. Results may be relatively poor.

It is usual that centroid is the mean value of the points in the cluster. The "nearest" is measured as Euclidean distance, cosine distance, correlation, etc. K-centers converge to the above-mentioned similarities.

Most of the convergence occurs in the first few iterations. Often the stop condition changes to "until relatively few points change the cluster."

Cluster analysis 52 Clustering using the K-environment algorithm. In the data set graph, you'll find that after five iterations on this example, centroids are "seamlessly shifted" (SciKit tolerance or threshold is in default state 0.0001).

After clustering has been completed, it is necessary to record centroids and cluster identity. Each new document is vectorized and compared with all the centroids. Centroid with the smallest distance from the new vectors post belongs to a cluster that we will assign to a new post.

The 20newsgroup is one of the "standard" data sets in the field of machine learning, which is often used to illustrate the cluster analysis (similar to what iris is used to illustrate the classification). It contains 18,826 posts from 20 different newsgroups, some of which are technical (comp.sys.mac.hardware, sci.crypt, and similar), while some relate to politics or religion. In our experiment, we will limit ourselves to technical ones. We will assume that each group is one cluster and examine whether our approach to finding linked posts works.

Module skleparn.datasets contains the function fetch_20newsgroups that automatically imports the following information:

>>> import sklearn.datasets

>>> all_data = sklearn.datasets.fetch_20newsgroups (subset = 'all')

>>> print (len (all_data.filenames)) 18846

>>> print (all_data.target_names) ['alt.atheism', 'comp.graphics',' comp.os.ms-windows.misc ',' comp.sys.ibm.pc.hardware ',' comp.sys .mac.hardware ',' comp.windows.x ',' misc.forsale ',' rec.autos ',' rec.motorcycles ',' rec.sport.baseball ',' rec.sport.hockey ',' sci .crypt, sci.electronics, sci.med, sci.space, soc.religion.christian, talk.politics.guns, talk.politics.mideast, talk.politics. .misc ',' talk.religion.misc '] Data set 59 Import of a meeting. If we want to import a separate training and test set, we do the following:

>>> train_data = conclude.datasets.fetch_20newsgroups (subset = 'train', categories = groups)

```
>>> print (len (train_data.filenames)) 11314
>>> test_data = sklearn.datasets.fetch_20newsgroups (subset
= 'test')
 >>> print (len (test_data.filenames)) 7532 We will limit
ourselves to a number of newsgroups by using the category
parameter as follows:
>>> groups = ['comp.graphics', 'comp.os.ms-windows.misc',
'comp.sys.ibm.pc.hardware', 'comp.sys.mac.hardware',
'comp.windows.x', 'sci.space'] >>> train_data =
concaten.datasets.fetch_20newsgroups (subset = 'train',
categories = groups)
>>> print ( len (train_data.filenames)) 3529
>>> test_data = sklearn.datasets.fetch_20newsgroups (subset
= 'test', categories = groups)
>>> print (len (test_data.filenames)) 2349 One thing should
always be taken into account - the actual data is silenced.
```

The data set we use is not an exception because it contains characters that can cause a UnicodeDecodeError error. Therefore, it should be noted that during the vectorization, these characters are ignored.

```
>>> vectorizer = StemmedTfidfVectorizer (min_df = 10,
max_df = 0.5, ... stop_words = 'english', decode_error =
'ignore')
>>> vectorized = vectorizer.fit_transform (train_data.data)
>>> num_samples, num_features = vectorized.shape
```

```
>>> print ("# samples:% d, #features:% d"% (num_samples,
num_features)) #samples: 3529, #features: 4712
```

This means that we have a set of 3,529 posts and that for each post feature vector we have formed a vector of 4,712 tags. These are the input data for the K-environment algorithm. We will set the number of clusters to 50 (for the exercise you can try other values for the number of clusters).

```
>>> num_clusters = 50 >>> from import.cnet import KMeans
>>> km = KMeans (n_clusters = num_clusters, init = 'random',
n_init = 1, verbose = 1, random_state = 3) >>> km.fit
(vectorized)
```

After the cluster, for each vectorized post we can extract the number of the cluster to which it belongs (integer value) using km.labels_. Centroids are available via km.cluster_centers_. >>> print (km.labels_) [48 23 31 ..., 6 2 22] >>> print (km.labels_.shape) 3529 New posts can be assigned to clusters using km.predict.

All that we have done so far will be used on the next post that is assigned to the new_post variable. "Disk drive problems. Hi, I have a problem with my hard drive. After 1 year, it works only sporadically now. I tried to format it, but now it does not boot anymore. Any ideas?

As mentioned before, we must vectorize the post before predicting the cluster. >>> new_post_vec = vectorizer.transform ([new_post]) >>> new_post_label = km.predict (new_post_vec) [0] The vector of the new post is not compatible with all posts, but only with those belonging to the same cluster. We will retrieve their indexes from the original dataset. >>> similar_indices = (km.labels _ == new_post_label) .nonzero () [0]

Comparison in brackets results in a string of Boolean values, and the nonzero () function converts the resulting string into a smaller string containing only True values.

Calculating the similarity (connection) of posts. We will create a list of all posts in the cluster and measure the similarity of existing posts with the new one. >>> similar = [] >>> for i in similar_indices: ... dist = sp.linalg.norm ((new_post_vec - vectorized [i]). toarray ()) ... similar.append ((dist, dataset .data [i])) >>> similar = sorted (similar) >>> print (len (similar)) 131

After computing the similarity, the most similar post can be displayed (placed in the show_at_1 variable), and in order to gain insight into the results of the similarity calculation, we will also show two less similar posts from the same cluster. >>> show_at_1 = similar [0] >>> show_at_2 = similar [int (len (similar) / 10)] >>> show_at_3 = similar [int (len (similar) / 2)]

The similarity of the post placed in the variable show_at_1 with the new post is 1,038 and the content is: BOOT PROBLEM with IDE controller Hi, I've got a Multi I / O card (IDE controller + serial / parallel interface) and two floppy drives (5 1/4 , 3 1/2) and a Quantum ProDrive 80AT connected to it. I was able to format the hard disk, but I could not boot from it. I can boot from drive A: (which disk drive does not matter) but if I remove the disk from drive A and press the reset switch, the LED of drive A: continues to glow, and the hard disk is not accessed at all. I guess this should be a problem of either the Multi I / O card or floppy disk drive settings (jumper configuration?) Does anyone have any hint what could be the reason for it. [...]

The similarity of the post placed in the variable show_at_2 with the new post is 1,150 and the content is: Booting from B drive I have a 5 1/4 "drive as drive A. How can I boot the system from my 3 1/2" B drive? (Optimally, the computer would be able to boot: from either A or B, checking them in order for a bootable disk. But: if I have to switch cables around and simply switch the drives so that: it cannot boot 5 1 / 4 "disks, that's OK. Also, boot_b will not do the trick for me. [...] Solving a given problem 70 Displaying relevant posts. The similarity of the post placed in the show_at_3 variable with the new post is 1,280 and the content is: IBM PS / 1 vs TEAC FD Hello, I've already tried our national without success. I tried to replace a friend with an original IBM floppy disk in his PS / 1-PC with a normal TEAC drive.

I have already identified the power supply on pins 3 (5V) and 6 (12V), shorted pin 6 (5.25 "/3.5" switch) and inserted pullup resistors (2K2) on pins 8, 26, 28, 30 and 34. The computer does not complain about a missing FD, but the FDs light is still on the clock.

The drive spins up ok when I insert a disc, but I cannot access it. The TEAC works fine in a normal PC. d? [...]

It is interesting how posts reflect the result of similarity measurements. The first post contains all the highlighted words from our new post. The second post also refers to a boot problem, but it's about floppy disks rather than hard drives. Finally, the third post does not even apply to the problem of booting or hard drives. However, we can notice that all three posts (including at least the same) belong to the same problem domain as the new post.

Is it realistic to expect perfect clustering? We cannot expect perfect clustering in the context that posts from the same group of news (for example, comp.graphics) are placed in the same cluster.

One of the reasons for this is noise. Please note the following post: >>> post_group = zip (train_data.data, train_data.target) >>> all = [(len (post [0]), post [0], train_data.target_names [post [1]]) for post and post_group] >>> graphics = sorted ([post for post in all if post [2] == 'comp.graphics']) >>> print (graphics [5]) (245,' From: SITUNAYA @ IBM3090.BHAM.AC.UK \ nSubject: test .... (sorry) \ nOrganization: The University of Birmingham, United Kingdom \ nLines: 1 \ nNNTP-Posting-Host: ibm3090.bham.ac.uk <... snip ...> ',' comp.graphics')

Are there indicators indicating that this post belongs to the group in which it is located? After preprocessing (tokenization, removing stop words and lowering the lower case), we get words that are not a sufficient indication that the post belongs to the comp.graphics group. "Standard" >>> noise_post = graphics [5] [1] >>> analyzer = vectorizer.build_analyzer () >>> print (list (analyzer (noise_post))) ['situnaya', 'ibm3090', 'bham' " " ", 'uk', 'subject', 'test', 'sorri', 'organ', 'univers', 'birmingham', 'unit', 'kingdom', 'line', 'nntp' post ',' host ',' ibm3090 ',' bham ',' ac ',' uk '] If we introduce additional filtering using parameters min_df and max_df, the situation gets worse because we get the following words: ac, birmingham, "Host", "kingdom", "nntp", "sorri", "test", "uk", "unit" and "univers".

The process of processing a collection of language documents is not trivial. In our case, data preprocessing is reduced to the conversion of text documents into numeric vectors suitable for clustering and similarity measurements. 2. Cluster analysis has shown that vectorized posts from the same problem domain (mostly) can be grouped into the same clusters, from which the measurement of similarity can distinguish posts related to the new one. 3. Data noise can negatively affect clustering performance. Experiment with the number of clusters, choosing initial centroid, clustering approaches based on other metrics!

Chapter 4

Modelling

❀ ı ❀ ı ❀ ı ❀ ı ❀ ı ❀ ı ❀ ı ❀ ı ❀ ı ❀ ı ❀ ı ❀ ı ❀ ı ❀ ı ❀

What is the difference between clustering and modeling?

In the previous chapter, we grouped textual documents using clustering. Each document after clustering belongs exactly to one cluster. However, suppose that we have a book that deals with machine learning and the Python programming language. We ask the question: what cluster should be put into the book - into a cluster where the machine learning books or clusters are grouped in which Python books are grouped?

In a classical bookstore, the book will be on a shelf in a window shop (that is, it is a topic in question). In the Internet Store, we can also label this book as a machine-learning book and as a book dealing with Python, which means it should be listed in two sections in an online bookstore (two topics). This does not mean that the book will be listed in all sections, for example, in a section that contains books on cooking, occultism, and the like.

What will we do at this time? This time, we will process methods that do not group documents into completely separate groups, but allow each document to refer to several topics, with topics automatically identified by a collection of text documents.

The subfield of machine learning that addresses this problem is called modeling of topics. Documents can be books or shorter texts like blogs, news, or emails. LDA is abbreviated from the English terms of the following methods: latent Dirichlet allocation, and linear discriminant analysis.

The methods relate to completely different things - modeling themes and classification, respectively. We will assume that we have the following sentences:

1. "I ate a banana and spinach smoothie for breakfast."

2. "I like to eat broccoli and bananas."

3. "Chinchillas and kittens are cute."

4. "My sister adopted a kitten yesterday. "

5. "Look at this cute hamster munching on a piece of broccoli."

LDA is a way to automatically detect topics that contain these sentences. For the preceding sentences and two themes, the LDA can produce the following: sentences 1 and 2 - 100% of topics A, sentences 3 and 4 - 100% of themes B, sentences 5 - 60% of themes A, 40% of themes B. topic A - 30% broccoli, 15% bananas, 10% breakfast, 10% munching, etc., so we can conclude that topic A refers to food, topic B - 20% chinchillas, 20% kittens, 20% cute,

15% hamster, etc. so we can conclude that topic B refers to animals. The question is, how does this actually work? The LDA "observes" the document as a mixture of topics on the basis of which words with different probabilities are generated.

The LDA is based on the assumption that each document in the collection is written as follows

- while writing a document, you: select the N number of the document that the document will have; select a mix of these themes (according to Dirihle's distribution in the final set of Elements)

- for example 1/3 refers to food, 2/3 per animal; you generate each word in a document by selecting a subject with a given probability (e.g., food with a probability of 1/3), then use the subject to generate a word (e.g. "broccoli" with a probability of 30%, "bananas" with a probability of 15%, etc. .)

This document generating model, LDA "reversing" finds a set of topics that most likely generated a collection of documents. For an example of generating a document d: Document d will have 5 words. Half of the document will refer to food and half to animals. The first word we choose from the topic that refers to food - "broccoli". The other word is chosen from the topic that refers to animals - "panda". The third word we choose from an animal-related theme - "adorable". The fourth word is chosen from the theme related to food - "cherries". The fifth word we choose from the theme related to food - "eating".

The document generated on the basis of the LDA model is "broccoli panda adorable cherries eating". As you can see, LDA is the so-called training with the collapsed Gibbs sampling method.

Suppose we have a collection of documents for which we want to discover K themes. We pass through each document and in a random way, we assign each word to one of the K topics.

Random assignments result in "not very meaningful" allocation of these documents and distribution of words with respect to themes, so the following algorithm is applied in order to make a meaningful assignment of these documents after a certain number of iterations. For each document d, each word w document d, and each topic t, calculate: $p(t \mid d)$ - the word relation in document d assigned to theme t, $ip(w \mid d)$ - the ratio of all documents containing the word w themes t. Assign a word to a new topic, where the theme t is chosen with the probability $p(t \mid d) \times p(w \mid d)$. On the basis of the generative model, we conclude that this is the probability that the topic t generated the word w so it is meaningful to replace the current theme that generated the word.

In other words, in this step, we assume that the links between topics and words are correct for all words except for the one we are currently processing, so that the current word is adapted. After a large number of iterations, a stable state with very good assignments is obtained.

We need a gensim package that supports LDA. You can install the package with the command: pip install gensim. Apart from the gensim package, we also need a set of data. We will use the Associated Press * news collection, which is often used in research related to topic modeling. After the download, the package is imported as follows:

```
>>> from gensim import corpora, models
>>> corpus = corpora.BleiCorpus ('./ data / ap / ap.dat',
'./data/ap/vocab.txt' ) Building a thematic model 13 Building a
model. A variable corpus contains all text documents in a
format suitable for further processing.
The model can be created using this object as input: model =
models.ldamodel.LdaModel (corpus, num_topics = 100,
id2word = corpus.id2word) The resulting model can be tested
in different ways, e.g.:
>>> doc = corpus.docbyoffset (0 )
 >>> topics = model [doc]
>>> print (topics) [(3, 0.023607255776894751), (13,
0.11679936618551275), .... (92, 0.10781541687001292)]
```

The result of the previous code is to a lesser extent different from each startup on the same data set, because random numbers are used in the training phase of the model. If we use themes to compare documents, then the algorithm is robust enough and changes are small. On the other hand, the sequence of different themes is quite chaotic.

We will generate a histogram from which you can see how many topics are assigned to documents. >>> num_topics_used = [len (model [doc]) for doc in corpus] >>> plt.hist (num_topics_used) Based on the histogram it can be seen that the largest number of documents are related to about 5 topics, and there are almost no documents related to more than 20 topics.

We ask the following question: why does the histogram look like this, or why do we link documents with a small number of themes? One of the main causes is the so-called alpha parameter. Without the "mathematics" orientation, the higher alpha parameter values will result in a greater number of topics that are relevant to the document.

The parameter value must be positive, but is usually set to a value of less than one. By default, the gensim will set the parameter value to 1 / num_topics, but it can be "manually" forwarded to the LdaModel constructor as follows: >>> model = models.ldamodel.LdaModel (corpus, num_topics = 100, id2word = corpus.id2word, alpha = 1) In the new histogram we made we can see that many documents are related to 20 to 25 different topics. If you reduce the value, the opposite will happen.

Technically, these are multinomial distributions, which means they assign the probability to each word in the dictionary. Words with high probability are more related to this topic than words with less probability. We will outline the words with the highest beliefs for several topics.

Theme no. Theme 1 dress military soviet president new state captured carlucci states leader stance government 2 koch zambia lusaka oneparty orange kochs party and government mayor new political 3 human turkey rights abuses royal thompson threats new state wrote garden president 4 bill employees experiments levin taxation federal measure legislation senate president whistleblowers sponsor 5 ohio july drought jesus disaster percent hartford mississippi crops northern valley virginia 6 united percent billion year president world years states states and bush news 7 b hughes affidavit states united ounces squarefoot care delaying charged unrealistic bush 8 yeutter dukakis bush convention farm subsidies uruguay percent general secretary i told 9 kashmir government people srinagar india dumps city two jammukashmir group moslem Pakistan 10 workers vietnamese irish wage immigrants percent bargaining last island police hutton I

Although at first glance it seems weird, when we read the list of words, we can clearly see that the topics are not just a list of random words, but that they are logical groups. We also see that these topics are related to older news, e.g. dated from time, the Soviet Union continued to exist, and Gorbachev was the Secretary General. We can also present themes as so-called Word clouds, in which words are more likely to be written as larger.

As an example, a cloud of words that relates to the Middle East and politics is easily found in the data set.

It is necessary to install pytagcloud.

```
# maxsize - the size of the largest word (int, optional),
fontname - the font name (e.g., word name, 'maxsize = 120,
fontname =' Lobster '):
# oname - output file, str, optional) from pytagcloud import
create_tag_image, make_tags # gensim returns the weight
between 0 and 1 for each word, and pytagcloud expects the
whole number.
# We multiply all large numbers and round off what is a good
approximation for this visualization. word = [(w, int (v *
10000)) tags = make_tags (words, maxsize = maxsize)
create_tag_image (tags, oname, size = (1800, 1200), fontname
= fontname)
```

From the word cloud it can be seen that some words should be removed (for example, the word "I"). Stop words do not contain as much information and do not need to give them the same meaning as words that do not appear often in different contexts. So, when modeling the topic, it is necessary to filter the stop word, otherwise a theme can be formed that consists exclusively of the stop word. In addition, it is necessary to normalize the word, i.e. to reduce the word to the form, for example, normalization of different forms of verbs.

After modeling themes, it is possible for each document to estimate how much of the document "emerge" from one topic, how much of the other, etc. This means that we can compare documents in "space space" (topic space). Simply put, instead of comparing the word, we say that the two documents are similar if they relate to the same topics. This is very useful in cases where two documents that contain several common words refer to the same topic using different constructions (for example, one document contains the "President of the United States", while the other contains "Donald Trump").

In other words, we no longer compare documents based on the word vector, but based on the theme vector (topic vector). We project documents into the theme space - that means we want to have vector topics that summarize the document. When topics are calculated for each document, we can perform operations on the theme vector and forget about the original words. If topics are important, they will be potentially more informative than raw words. Additionally, this can lead to a decrease in total computation when comparing the vector, as the much faster comparison of 100 vectors containing the weight of the theme, than the vector containing thousands of terms, is much faster.

```
>>> from gensim import matutils
>>> topics = matutils.corpus2dense (model [corpus],
num_terms = model.num_topics)
>>> from scipy.spatial import distance >>> pairwise =
distance.squareform (distance.pdist (topics ))
>>> largest = pairwise.max () >>> for you in range (len (topics)):
pairwise [ti, ti] = largest + 1 >>> def closest_to (doc_id): return
pairwise [doc_id] .argmin ()
```

Variable topics is a matrix theme. We calculate the distance between each other using the SciPy pdist function.With one function call, we count all values: sum ((topics [ti] - topics [tj]) ** 2). The diagonal matrix elements are set to a value greater than any value in the matrix. Can you guess why this is necessary? The closest_to function works similar to the methods of the nearest neighbors. From: geb@cs.pitt.edu (Gordon Banks) Subject: Re: Request for information on "essential tremor" and Indrol? In article

<1q1tbnINNnfn@life.ai.mit.edu> sundar@ai.mit.edu writes:

Essential tremor is a progressive hereditary tremor that gets worse when a patient tries to use the affected member. All limbs, vocal cords, and head can be involved. Inderal is a beta-blocker and is usually effective in decreasing the tremor. Alcohol and mysoline are also effective, but alcohol is too toxic to use as a treatment. ----- ---   ---------------------------

Gordon Banks N3JXP, geb@cadre.dsl.pitt.edu | "Skepticism is the chastity of the intellect, and it is shameful to surrender it too soon."
-- ---------------------------

If we ask for the most similar document to the previous one, the closest_to_ (1) will return the post by the same author in which the medicines are also considered.

From: geb@cs.pitt.edu (Gordon Banks)

Subject: Re: High   Prolactin   In   article
<93088.112203JER4@psuvm.psu.edu>   JER4@psuvm.psu.edu
(John E. Rodway) writes:>

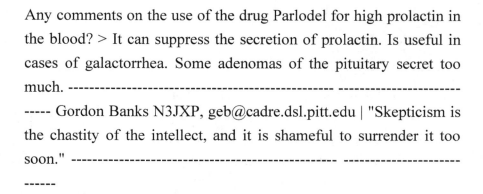

Any comments on the use of the drug Parlodel for high prolactin in the blood? > It can suppress the secretion of prolactin. Is useful in cases of galactorrhea. Some adenomas of the pituitary secret too much. --- ---------------------- ----- Gordon Banks N3JXP, geb@cadre.dsl.pitt.edu | "Skepticism is the chastity of the intellect, and it is shameful to surrender it too soon." --- ---------------------- ------

The initial implementation of the LDA are slow (the original algorithm was published in scientific work in 2003), which limits their use to small collection of documents. However, modern algorithms work well with a very large collection of data (a method that we will use to further process Wikipedia was created in 2010). Following the documentation of the gensim package, we will create a thematic model for a part of Wikipedia in English. Note that this is feasible on your laptop, but it's time-consuming. First download the Wikipedia dump file (note that this is a file size of several GB): https://dumps.wikimedia.org/enwiki/latest/enwiki-latest-pages-articles.xml.bz2. Then it is indexed using a gensim tool, calling from the command line rather than from the Python shell: python -m gensim.scripts.make_wiki enwiki-latest-pages-articles.xml.bz2 wiki_en_output After a while, the index will be generated in the same directory.

After that, we import the gensim package and event recording package: >>> import logging, gensim We record events by using the standard Python logging module (which genism uses to display status messages). This step is not mandatory, but in cases where data processing takes a long time, it is desirable to get some information about what's going on.

```
>>> logging.basicConfig (format = '% (asctime) s:%
(levelname) s:% (message) s', level = logging.INFO)
 We load the pre-processed data in the following way:
>>> id2word = gensim.corpora.Dictionary.load_from_text
('wiki_en_output_wordids.txt')
```

>>> mm = gensim.corpora.MmCorpus ('wiki_en_output_tfidf.mm') We create LDA model as before. Please note that this operation takes a long time. At the console you will see which part of the work done by the algorithm, which allows you to conclude how much longer you will wait.

>>> model = gensim.models.ldamodel.LdaModel (corpus = mm, id2word = id2word, num_topics = 100, update_every = 1, chunksize = 10000, passes = 1) How can we preserve the model? After generating a model, you can record it using the save () method so that you do not repeat the process.

>>> model.save ('wiki_lda.pkl') The model can be loaded in the new session as follows: >>> model = gensim.models.ldamodel.LdaModel.load ('wiki_lda.pkl')

Although we had significantly more documents than in the previous case (about 4 million in 2015), the model is still of the type sparse.

```
>>> print (np.mean (lens)) 6.41
>>> print (np.mean (lens <= 10)) 0.941
```
This means that an average document associated with 6.4 topics and that 94% of documents are associated with 10 or fewer topics. What is the most common topic in Wikipedia? We will ask the following question: What is most talked about in Wikipedia? First, we will calculate the total weight for each topic (adding the weight of all documents) and then extract the words relevant to the subject. We can do this with the following code:

```
>>> weights = topics.sum (axis = 0)
>>> words = model.show_topic (weights.argmax (), 64)
```
After visualization we see that music The most widely used topic - about 18% of Wikipedia's pages are related to this topic, and about 5.5% of all Wikipedia's words are assigned to this topic. * The word cloud for Wikipedia is plotted based on data from 2015. Since Wikipedia is constantly changing, most likely you will get a different cloud of words.

What is the topic least present on Wikipedia? If argmax () is replaced with argmin (), we get the word cloud for the least present topic.

```
>>> words = model.show_topic (weights.argmin (), 64)
```
The least talked about is harder to interpret. Some of the most significant words point to airports in eastern countries. About 1.6% of documents refer to this topic, and less than 0.1% of all the words in Wikipedia are assigned to this topic.

Does the number of them significantly affect the final outcome? So far, we have used a fixed number of topics for our analyzes - 100. It was a quite arbitrary number - we could have used 20 or 200 topics. For many purposes, this number is not too important. If we use the topics only as a middle step (like when looking for similar posts), the final behavior of the system is rarely more sensitive to the exact number of topics used in the model.

This means that as long as you use enough topics, whether you use 100 or 200, the recommendations that come out of the process will not be much different. 100 topics are often quite good choices, while 20 are too small for a general collection of text documents. The same is true for setting the value of the alpha parameter - during the experiment with it the subject may change, but the final results are robust against this change.

Final notes 41 Automatically determine the number of topics. There are several methods that will automatically determine the number of topics depending on the data set. One of the models is a hierarchical Dirichlet process. Unlike the LDA, where the number of topics is fixed, in this case the themes are generated together with the data - one by one. Generally, this means the following: the more documents, the more topics.

Chapter 5

Activation Functions for Modeling

❈ ❈ ❈ ❈ ❈ ❈ ❈ ❈ ❈ ❈ ❈ ❈ ❈ ❈ ❈ ❈

In Python, activation functions can be used for building neural networks. The inclusion of these functions is important because they sort out which neuron in the network is used for what when an output is created. The output of the neurons and which information passes through which neurons are also dictated by these functions. An action function is a transformation that starts in the input layer where the output of the layer is used as input in the others.

Popular Activation Functions

Binary Step Function

This function is threshold-based. It is a classifier that dictates if a networks calculation process could use a neuron. The neuron is activated if its output value is greater than the given threshold. If it is not the neuron should not be activated.

The basic form of the function is :f(x) = 1, x>=0.

This is an example of a simple activation function. This one can be used if a binary classifier needs to be made.

63

Sigmoid function

The sigmoid function is another simple activation function. Most engineers use this when they are developing a deep neural network. The examples of the sigmoid function that you find in books is used to activate the layers in the network. The functions form is:$f(x) = 1/(1+e^{-x})$.

The function itself is continuously differentiable, smooth and non-linear. By non-linear, it is implied that a non-linear output comes out when you multiply the number of neurons that have the function. The output value comes in the range between 0 and 1, where 1 and 0 are included and the diagram is drawn in an S shape.

Tanh

The tanh function is fairly similar to the sigmoid function, as the tanh function is a scaled version of the sigmoid function. The following function gives you the end result: $tanh(x) = 2sigmoid(2x)-1$.

The function can be written in the following way as well: $tanh(x)=2/ (1+e^{(-2x)})-1$. Dissimilar to the sigmoid function, the tanh function is symmetric. This solves the issue that the end values will be of the same sign. Similar to the sigmoid function, tanh is continuous at all points and differentiable. Being non-linear, it makes it easier for the engineers to backpropagate errors.

ReLU

The Rectified Linear Unit, also known as ReLU function has the following form: $f(x)=max(0,x)$. While designing networks this function is widely used. It is a nonlinear function, meaning that backpropagation of errors and activating several layers of neurons are all possible. Not having to activate every neuron in the network is one of the advantages of working with ReLU. This means that it will deactivate a neuron and convert its output to zero if it's negative. The networks will be sparse in this case and computing the problem will be much easier.

Choosing the Right Activation Function

Learning when each activation function can be used and what it does in the situation is the next thing you should learn after you have gotten to know them better. Depending on the properties of a problem you can determine which activation is the best for the situation.

- Classification problems are solved by the Sigmoid function and its combinations.

- If you want to avoid the problem of the vanishing gradient you should not use the Sigmoid Activation function and its variants.

Chapter 6

Past The Math

❀ ꙳ ❀ ꙳ ❀ ꙳ ❀ ꙳ ❀ ꙳ ❀ ꙳ ❀ ꙳ ❀ ꙳ ❀ ꙳ ❀ ꙳ ❀ ꙳ ❀

W e're done! There will be little to no math from this point onwards. You've already hopefully understood the fundamentals of ML, and your mathematical foundation seems strong enough to keep going.

Keeping Training and Test Data Separate

When it comes to supervised learning, you need to provide the machine with a training dataset. It needs to contain labels and the objects they present. You need to show the machine how some labels are tied to objects. Then, you input a larger validation dataset of objects that aren't connected to the labels so that you can gauge how the machine deals with new objects. You tell the machine when it makes a mistake and when it makes a good choice.

This way the machine can adjust and fine-tune. Keep in mind that the validation dataset is only a part of a larger training set and is designed specifically for fine-tuning of the parameters in the network. The database you use for the test is only used for the measurement of the final performance.

Inexperienced teams tend to combine training and test data in order to improve the results of their model. This way they allow the machine access to some of the answers. This approach does improve the results, however, performance is impaired due to the machine lacking the ability to adjust the weights and biases. The improvement can be minor and quite superficial. It's hardly ever worth it. You can compare this to a student using cheats on a test. He might do well on the test, but his knowledge will be scarce.

What you should take from this is that it's a bad idea to mix the two types of data. They should always be separate

Carefully Choosing Your Training Data

Machines are comparable to humans when it comes to learning in the way that they can encounter a mental block sometimes. Feeding the machine training data that is not tied to test data can give you a false positive and you might end up misguided on the performance of your machine. It is similar to multiplication. If you teach someone how to multiply single-digit numbers and ask them to solve problems which concern the multiplication of numbers with more digits, their results are bound to suffer. In a similar way, you should make sure that your training data is representative of the data you will use after and during the testing.

Make sure that you don't select the data with your own bias. Let's say that you are trying to develop a model that can predict the results of voting around the country. If you only feed the machine data concerning how white, middle-aged women form a certain vote, the program is bound to do poorly. In short, if the data you provide the machine with only considers a limited set of parameters, it will not do well in testing.

Taking an Exploratory Approach

Supervised machine learning is a great tool that can help answer specific questions, as well as solve specific problems. Due to this, most organizations tend to ignore the potential that lies in exploring unsupervised learning. This valuable tool is left under-utilized as it is hard to conceptualize and artificial network that can recognize patterns that aren't inputted by hand.

While it may be tempting to view machine learning as another project. There are more intricacies to it than you may realize at first. You do not want your teams to just spit out reports. What you are looking to do is find a way to find patterns in the data that may help you figure out how what the next innovative idea is, as well as help you see the problems that you weren't aware of or never looked for.

Choosing the Right Tool for the Job

While machine learning is indeed a powerful tool, you will see that it is not the only tool. Sometimes, you can fetch the information you want in easier ways, like looking at a graph or table or by simply talking to people from different places. You should never simply assume that machine learning is the best way for solving all problems and answering all questions.

Besides certain things in Machine Learning not being stabilized, Machine Learning does not have that many problems. It is hard to remember that Machine Learning is still in its infancy and is still being trained as technology evolves, so we must be patient and keep in mind that there are going to be more problems before they are to be fixed.

Unsolved Problems

As we have already stated, Machine Learning is changing together with technology, so it is likely that there will come a time when you will not have any issues to deal with before finding an answer. Even now, people are working on developing a way around these issues. Even if these efforts prove fruitless you will have ways to analyze data and get the wanted results without any issues. A few issues that Machine Learning hasn't been able to solve are listed below.

The first problem revolves around the variable event space. This problem has yet to be solved as a classification system that is able to respond in an efficient and meaningful way is going to be needed, regardless of the training data.

Another problem is the lack of contextual understanding while processing languages. Machine Learning heavily relies on context analysis to function because it allows for a lot of things to be misunderstood. One of the solutions is that the open AI team could come up with some sort of solution that helps the agents with the creation of their own rules, as opposed to making a situation where it is necessary to find patterns.

Facial identification is becoming more and more popular as a way for people to unlock their phones or other devices as it is quick and is a semi-secure way to prevent potential hackings of the device. However, it has many flaws. For example, people with facial features similar to yours can easily get into your phone. Another problem is that facial recognition does not account for make-up. This makes it difficult for women to unlock their phone due to a slight alteration in appearance.

Automated learning is one of the basic principles for the function of Machine Learning, and if a machine can't learn what it is supposed to do automatically, then it will fail to be useful to the company that uses it. Learning has to be drawn out from different resources, and when a graph is formed based on a connected sense that is found to be missing, then the automated learning will hit a snag and will have many gaps in its functions. IBM's Watson, for example, has done an excellent job so far, but a system that is geared for automated intelligence is still needed.

In some Machine Learning, you will see the machine in a position where it has to make decisions based on its reasoning on a test space that deviates: this, however, is not inclusive of rule-based engines. Machine Learning will need space for reasoning and debatable agents that will assist the reasoning are required to make the reasoning itself.

If you ever talked to Siri and got her confused while saying something to her or while saying something to someone else, you encountered an issue that Machine Learning has when it comes to repose generation. To be more accurate, Siri is unable to create a contextual response while you talk to her unless the response is already programmed or if the problem can be looked up on the internet.

Machine Learning has an issue with the three-way human rule too. Machines are not always capable of comprehending the knowledge that humanity functions under a three-way rule that gives a type and description to an image. If Machine Learning surpassed this issue, it would be able to classify art, music, and other subjects.

Another issue arises when it comes to memory networks. Despite the fact that it is a common belief that working with technology does not require a lot of space, this is not the case. In order to store all of the collected data a lot of space needs to be available.

As machines are not people they cannot come up with the thoughts that people can. However, it is possible to teach machines, not when we push them to the limits, but where we let them grow to the point where human input is not needed. While technology is bound to have some holdups, eventually they will be solved. One of the possible reasons for not finding the solution yet is that our technology is not advanced enough.

Some Problems that can be Solved

Machine Learning helps many companies and individuals with their daily activities. In the following chapter, you will be presented with a few points that were touched upon as problems that have yet to be solved by Machine Learning. It does not mean that the machine learning does not work if it has some of those problems, however. Sometimes, an issue can be patched and fixed later, after the issues were discovered by the users. There can always be some problems that the developers didn't account for in the software and the only real way to find them is through the users themselves.

Spam detection is helped by Machine Learning. When you access your inbox, you will notice emails that are automatically routed to your spam box because of certain keywords that the program detected in other emails. Still, some spam gets through because the keywords have been found in the inbox. It is filtering those keywords into your inbox for the unlikely, yet possible, occurrence that you may want the email even though it is spam. Spam detection can evolve further in many ways, but it is comforting to see that it's getting better and better.

Lately, credit card companies have been keeping a close eye on unauthorized usage of credit cards. If someone else used it, you will be alerted as soon as possible. How is that possible? They do this with the help of the transaction record. The credit card knows about how much you spend monthly and if there is any sort of activity in places where you usually do not make purchases or more than predicted is spent, they are going to assume that your card was stolen and it will be reported. This can cause some problems if you go on a trip or if you spend more money than you usually would.

Machine Learning is starting to be able to recognize zip codes on envelopes to make the process of sorting them out easier by dividing the envelopes based on geographic location allowing them to be sorted and delivered faster. It is not perfect, but it's making steady progress. The main issue is the fact that machines can have trouble reading certain handwritings. This is a problem because everyone writes differently.

As we have touched upon, Siri is capable of understanding you. Wouldn't it be great if other machines could do this? Thanks to Machine Learning, this is becoming reality slowly, but steadily. The main problem here is that Machine Learning interacts poorly with dialects and different languages. Aside from that, the dictionary is evolving rapidly and the machine can't keep up. Even with these issues, however this does not stop the machine from trying to fulfill your request.

While uploading a picture onto Facebook, you might be asked if you want to tag a person if a face is recognized on the photo. This is great for sharing memories and experiences, as well as connecting with others. This also allows the person to know if they want it on their profile or not. It works on the same principle as the algorithm that unlocks your screen via facial recognition.

It is common knowledge that while you log into some websites like Amazon, you are presented with a list of products that you may be interested in. These offers are extracted from your past purchases and the links you have visited. The algorithm looks for keywords and similarities and uses them to form a personalized shopping experience that is unique to only you. In order to achieve this, Amazon and similar websites use the same algorithm in order to keep you coming back. You can see this algorithm in many other different places such as Facebook where it allows Facebook to access other websites so that it may engage you with ads you might want to see, as the generic ones tend to be not very engaging.

The field of medicine must constantly evolve so it does not fall behind. Machine Learning can be used to take the symptoms a patient is suffering from. With this, they can plug these symptoms into a computer and get several different diagnoses. The system isn't perfect, but it is going to give the healthcare provider a direction to think in so that they may give an accurate diagnosis for the patient.

If you ever dabble in stocks, there is one thing that you should focus on more than anything else. Knowing when to trade and when to hold on to the stocks is key to making money. Machine Learning has created an algorithm that takes financial information and analyzes it in order to help the brokers know when trading or keeping stocks is the better choice. This helps plenty of companies save money by preventing them from buying useless stock or keeping stock whose price is about to plummet.

Duplication and inaccurate data can be fairly common issues when the data is input by humans. With Machine Learning, however, algorithms work based on predictive modeling in order to fix these issues. They can learn to deal with extensive documentation and data entry tasks. This is a big help to people who want to focus more on problem-solving and don't want to waste time with menial labor. This makes the process more efficient and the machine will do a better job with the data than a human could.

Dulight is an amazing invention created by Baidu that helps people who are visually handicapped to learn about their surroundings. A computer with image recognition will be used to survey the space around them and then transmit it to them through an earpiece that tells them what they would see. It is a truly marvelous invention that is surely going to improve many lives.

Most companies in the world that are in business use Machine Learning extensively. Though it is not used in a way that can be seen by the general public or the employees, it is used in even the simplest of jobs like analyzing data. This helps better their decisions aimed towards gaining money.

Chapter 7

Other Applications of Machine Learning

❋ ❙ ❋ ❙ ❋ ❙ ❋ ❙ ❋ ❙ ❋ ❙ ❋ ❙ ❋ ❙ ❋ ❙ ❋ ❙ ❋ ❙ ❋ ❙ ❋ ❙ ❋

In this chapter, we take a look at some theoretically more complex portions of ML from a theoretical standpoint. Rather than killing you with math, I opted to give you a foundation, and then go into theory.

Machine Learning and Reversions

In statistical modeling, you might notice that reversion analysis aims to be a process which helps estimate the various relationships between different variables. This will include several techniques that are typically used for variable analysis and matching when several variables are worked with at once whenever you are showing the relationship between independent and dependent variables.

Reversion analysis is a valuable tool when it comes to understanding how the usual value for variable changes over time. Reversion will also help you estimate the conditional expectation of a variable that depends on the independent variable and the average value of said variable. Briefly put, It will shorten the time you spend while juggling multiple values.

More uncommon are situations where you will be presented with a variable that depends on the independent variable along with its quantile or location parameters for the conditional distribution. Usually, the estimate you come to will be an expression for the independent value. We call this the reversion expression. In reversion analysis, you will be showing your interest in the characterization of the variation of the dependent variable in relation to the expression which we can describe as the probability distribution.

One of the possible approaches is taking a conditional analysis. This will take the estimate for the maximum over the average for the dependent variables, which are, again, based on the independent variable that is given. This allows you to determine if the independent variable is necessary or sufficient for the value that the dependent variable holds.

You will use reversion when you are looking to forecast and when it overlaps with machine learning. It will be a good tool for when you are trying the relationships between dependent and independent variables. When dealing with a restricted circumstance, reversion will be used to infer the causal relationship between the variables. You should be cautious, however, as it may give you a false relationship.

There are several different techniques for reversion. Linear reversion and least squares diversion are two of them. Your reversion expression will be defined as finite numbers which don't have a parameter. Nonparametric reversion is a tool that we will be utilizing when we want to permit the reversion expression to be used as a collection of expressions for infinite dimensionality.

Your performance when it comes to revision analysis is going to be a summary of the methods that you practice as processes for data generation and how it ties back into the reversion approach that you applied. The true form of data generation is not always going to be known as reversion analysis and depends on the extent of your assumptions.

The assumptions you provide will need to be testable so you can see if you have provided the machine with enough data.

Machine Learning and Robotics

I believe that we have helped you grow more familiar with what machine learning is. It should not surprise you that it sparked an interest in robotics and has stayed roughly the same for the past several years. But are robots related to machine learning?

Robotics has not developed too much in the past several years. However, these developments are a great foundation for discoveries to come and some even relate to machine learning.

When it comes to robotics, the following five applications apply in machine learning:

1.Computer vision: some would say that robot vision and machine vision are more correct as far as terminology goes. For a very long time, engineers and roboticists have been trying to develop a type of camera that will let a robot process the physical world around him as data. Robot vision and machine vision are two terms that go hand in hand. Their creation can be credited to the existence of automated inspection systems and robot guidance. The two have a very small difference and it comes in regards to kinematics in the use of robot vision. It encompasses the calibration of the comment frame and enhances the robot's ability to affect its surroundings physically.

The already impressive advances in computer vision that have been instrumental in coming up with techniques that are geared for prediction learning, has been further helped by a huge influx of data.

2. Imitation learning: this is relatively closely connected to observational learning. It is common with kids and has common features, the most obvious being probabilistic models and Batesian. The main question, however, stands. Will it find use in humanoid robots?

Imitation learning has always been an important part of robotics as it has features of mobility that transcend those of factory settings in domains like search and rescue construction, which makes the programming robotic solutions manually a puzzle.

3. Self-Supervised learning: Allows robots to generate their training instance due to the self-supervised learning approaches, in order to improve their performance. This includes priority training, as well as data that is captured and is used to translate vague sensor data. The robots with optical devices that have this installed can reject and detect objects.

A solid example called Watch-Bot has been created by Cornell and Stanford. It utilized a laptop and laser pointer, a 3D sensor, and a camera in order to find normal human activities like patterns that are learned through the methods of probability. A laser pointer is used to detect the distance to the object. Humans are notified 60 percent of the time, as the robot has no concept of what he is doing and why he is doing it.

4. Medical and assistive technologies: A device that senses and oversees the processing of sensory information before setting an action that is going to benefit a senior or someone with incapacities. This is the basic definition of the assistive robot. They have a capacity for movement therapy, as well as the ability to provide other therapeutic and diagnostic benefits. They are quite cost-prohibitive for hospitals in the US and abroad, so they still haven't left the lab.

Robotics in the field of medicine has advanced at a rapid rate even though they are not used by medical facilities. This advancement can be seen clearly if you see the capabilities of these robots.

5. Multi-Agent learning: It offers some key components such as negotiation and coordination. This involves that the robot, based on machine learning, finds equilibrium strategies and adapts to a shifting landscape.

During late 2014, an excellent example of an algorithm used by distributed robots or agents was made in one of MIT's labs for decision and information systems. The robots collaborated and opted to build a more inclusive and better learning model than that which was done by a single robot. They did so via building exploration and teaching them to find the quickest ways through the rooms in order to construct a knowledge base in an autonomous manner.

Every robot makes catalogs which they combine with the datasets of the others. The standard algorithm is outperformed here and the distributed algorithm comes into play when it comes to making knowledge bases like this one. This sort of approach, while by no means faultless, will allow robots to relate catalogs and reinforce their explanations while fixing any omissions and overgeneralizations. This all plays a great part in multiple robotic applications in the near future.

Catalogs are made by every robot which they then combine to the datasets of other robots, where the standard algorithm is outperformed by the distributed algorithm when making this sort of knowledge base. This sort of machine learning approach, while not a faultless system, is going to allow robots to relate the catalogs and reinforce mutual explanations while correcting any omissions or overgeneralizations, which will play a role in multiple robotic applications in the near future.

What do ads do? They pop up from time to time on our devices, broadcasts and mailboxes. Wherever you look you are at risk of them popping up and bugging you with something that you are not interested in. This shows just how impersonal companies tend to be. As they bombard you with ads hoping that at least one will hit. These companies do not know any better and continue to pay big money in order to keep up this kind of marketing. You will notice how embarrassing, wacky, and bizarre the ads can be and they are almost never welcome. There is one thing we can hope for when it comes to ads. Machine learning is bringing a time when cheap ads that are tailored to our behavior will be shown to us in the best time. Algorithms that function like that are already being made.

There is one thing that has been proven in regards to consumer behavior: people purchase things automatically. While people are unlikely to change their buying habits, it's possible that there could be some major life events that can shake them up. This means that a company that deals with candy does not aim it's marketing to people who would never try their products. Instead, they target people who could try them due to some life event like divorce, pregnancy, or whatever else that could get someone to purchase candy. How do these companies know which person likes what? Data mining is the tool used here. It gathers data on people so that computers can analyze what you want, like, or motivates you so that they can target you with ads that are good for you. Obviously, the ads are not very good at persuading you, so machines have to learn to be persuasive and manage to do so as demonstrated below.

In 2012 an article named "How Companies Learn Your Secrets" came out in the *New York Times*. It talks about a man named Andrew Pole, who is a statistician that worked at Target in 2002. His job was gathering up data about customers by aggregating, or, at times, even purchasing packages of personal data. This can include the cars they drive, what topics they are concerned about online and small things like the brand of orange juice they use. This is made possible because machines analyzing the customer's data is not technically a violation of someone's privacy. None of the information is read or tampered with by humans working in Target. On top of that, every single one of the customers is tagged under a number instead of a name. The users' personal information isn't made public, so there is no law by which this is considered illegal.

At one moment, Andrew tried to find out which women visiting their store were pregnant so he could push them towards buying products that people with kids would purchase. Women outing themselves as being pregnant by buying baby shower products in the store gave Andrew information that he fed to machine learning which gave Andrew a list of 25 products. Amongst these products, there were cotton balls, zinc supplements, and similar products. This gave him the idea of how long the woman was pregnant and how long she has until giving birth. This information was then used so that Target could push the products they sell to the woman when it is most needed by her. Based on her marital status, if she shops online, and many other factors gave the computers in Target the chance to skim the data and provided likelihood for the woman to become a regular shopper for baby-related products.

The same logic was then applied to all of the female shoppers in Target and eventually came to the point where they could, with a high degree of accuracy, concur which women are pregnant without having that information revealed to anyone. This was a scandal just waiting to spread, similar to what happened with Cambridge Analytica. However, Target saw this as a great opportunity for getting new customers.

This is exactly how major corporations want things to play out. Operating in morally grey areas, as well as creatively skipping around privacy laws so that they can get an advantage over their competitors is not something that is uncommon in the world of business. Similar situations could play out easily, but, this time, if one woman revealed everything about herself, the privacy of other women would start to be affected. This brings us to a conclusion. There is a parameter when we look at a society where a single person's habits are easy to ignore relatively to a large enough group of people as general behavior applies to everyone. For data mining to be completely snuffed out we are going to have to do it all together. If we start avoiding Target, Walmart and similar chains and start shopping online, we will not prevent data mining as the most powerful medium miners will stay. We can't run away from social networks.

Chapter 8

Artificial Intelligence

❀ ❀ ❀ ❀ ❀ ❀ ❀ ❀ ❀ ❀ ❀ ❀ ❀ ❀ ❀ ❀ ❀ ❀

Over the last few years, many advancements regarding AI were made. You can see robots in different science fiction movies doing an amazingly vast assortment of actions and with impressive accuracy. Such a thing would be amazing to have today, wouldn't it? AI is the first step towards something like that. Artificial Intelligence is sprouting everywhere around us. Siri and Google Assistant are examples of that. They can offer us advice or recommendations based on our habits. They improve every year so that they may increase the capacity to recognize images, voices and even evolve as far as performing more complicated actions such as driving cars by applying techniques that Deep Learning uses. Another way these systems are growing is that we are bringing them closer and closer to understanding language and communicating.

The AI craze has brought about a load of confusion as many companies are starting to delve into the scene. How do we understand all of this?

The simplest definition of AI suggests that it is a specific field of computer science that aims to develop computers which perform tasks typically done by people. Specifically, the jobs done by highly intelligent people.

AI, also known as Artificial Intelligence, is called machine intelligence as well. It is the intelligence seen in machines and aims to mimic the natural intelligence which people function with. In computer science, AI research is defined as a study of intelligence in machines that can perceive their surroundings in order to increase their chances of reaching their goal. Usually, the term AI is usually connected to machine learning that aims to copy a human's function, learning or problem-solving. The term itself is more encompassing than that however and has many definitions depending on which science is talking about them.

"AI is whatever hasn't been done yet" is a fairly popular quote that people like to talk about. It was a quip made by Tesler when discussing the AI phenomenon where people often forget about AI being able to use its intelligence for completing tasks while defining it. Modern machines can now perform things that may classify them as AI due to the ability to understand speech and beating human opponents in highly strategical games like go and chess. They can do many other incredible things, as well, such as dealing with routing when it comes to content delivery or in military simulations.

Artificial intelligence, otherwise known as AI, is often referred to as machine intelligence and it is the intelligence that is commonly shown in machines as opposed to the natural intelligence that is usually seen in humans and various other mammals. When it comes to computer science, artificial intelligence research is going to be listed as a study of intelligence that is shown by devices that can perceive the environment around it in order to take actions that can maximize its chances of being successful in reaching its goals. Informally, the word artificial intelligence will usually be linked to a machine that can copy a human's cognitive function problem-solving or learning.

AI had many great runs. During the sixties, great promises regarding what machines can do were made. During the eighties, people started talking about how this could revolutionize everything. These two eras made promises that might have been too difficult to deliver upon. You might be wondering what makes this era different. Why are the systems that were made recently different from the programs that were made in the sixties and eighties? The new developments are different than the previous for many different reasons.

Increased Computational Resources

The computers in modern times function at much greater speeds and can do many more things and at far greater efficiency. The techniques from the past worked on their own only at that time, while, today, they can be used to improve and expand the computational grid.

Growth of Data

Until now, a great amount of data was collected and continues to grow. This data is becoming more and more available to machines. This has given our machines more potential things to think about. This shows us that the systems are getting better and better when it comes to understanding large amounts of data.

Deeper Focus

Smaller aspects of data are far below the abilities of AI which, now, focuses on solving entire problems. The systems we have today can think about particular problems. They don't work on daydreams anymore. Cortana, Siri, and other similar systems are good at functioning in limited domains and are focused on finding and pulling specific words that you might say instead of focusing on the sentence as a whole.

Knowledge Engineering

Problems and issues that knowledge engineering has faced now function as aspects of learning. The systems of today have their own ways of learning. The failures of the systems in the past help us build upon that knowledge in order to avoid those problems when it comes to processing data. Learning these rules without human input is what most of the approaches of today focus on.

Alternative Reasoning Models

Machines not having to reason in order to be smart is a basis for some alternative reasoning models. This assumption separates the machine from human beings and lets it work like a machine.

The first renaissance of intelligent machines comes from the previous factors. These machines are becoming more and more wide spread and are becoming better adopted in workplaces as tools.

Exploring AI

Some researchers and developers opt to make a system that can think and act as similarly to humans as possible. Most people don't care about how the systems think, they only worry about the morality of the system. Between these two ways of thinking are many that are not as extreme. If human reasoning is applied to systems it might help computers behave more like humans.

Strong AI

Strong AI is the term we use for work that simulates human reasoning within a machine. It dictates that any machine should be able to have the same capabilities and the same results as human beings. In order to achieve this, we will have to build some complex simulations that emulate human cognition and minds.

Weak AI

Weak AI is a term we come to when we talk about the second school of thought, which is trying to just get the structures to work.

Weak AI is able to create structures that are the same in function, but tell us nothing about how people think or feel. An example of this is Deep Blue, made by IBM. It is a gadget that managed to beat many professional chess players. Despite this success, it is obvious that we learned nothing about cognition in general.

Anything in Between

All of the nodes between Strong AI and Weak AI are those that understand reasoning but don't let it constrain their possibilities. The most powerful work happens in this group. Here, human emotions and reasoning are not the end goal for modeling the system, but a guide for achieving it. There is no fully accepted name for this school of thought. Practical AI is used relatively commonly.

What you should conclude from this is that the system needs to be smart, but not necessarily in the same way a human would be.

The Ecosystem around AI

Artificial Intelligence has been a thing for a very long time. Even though the interest   AI decrease and increase in intervals, it has always been around us. Even though some systems are smart and efficient, they are hard to consider AI. They are called narrow because they function exactly according to expectations. However, efficiency and smartness are a more important aspect.

Understanding that AI is everywhere

Suggestions that sites like Amazon and eBay give usually implement something that is very close to the human condition. These websites generate lists by means of data mining. By analyzing what you purchased in the past, as well as what you bookmarked or viewed, they will suggest products that are similar to what you looked at. They often find people with similar interests to yours and look into products they have purchased and recommends them to you. It is a process very similar to human thinking, even though not identical. For example, if you are trying to find a gift for your friend, you will start by thinking about what your friend likes or dislikes. Based on that information, you will find a gift that seems good for your friend. Another way to do it is to find someone with similar interests and ask them what they would like if they were in your friend's place.

You should not think about how these engines work at the moment. Grading them as good or bad should not matter. Instead, you should be impressed by how capable the engines are of generating profiles, identifying similarities between people, and generating suggestion lists based on information.

What makes human beings so smart?

Intelligence and thinking, to put it simply, can be defined into three stages:

- Taking the information in

- Reasoning

- Acting

There are further distinctions that we can make about these broad terms. Below, we will further talk about each of these actions.

Sensing

This process is one of the simplest to explain. It is responsible for collecting the information from our surroundings. Image sensing and speech sense are the two most common methods of doing this.

Image Processing

Differentiating between people, objects and other entities based on sight is done this way. One of the most basic survival skills humans have is their ability to perceive information around them.

Speech Recognition

The most basic way of transferring information from one person to another is through speech. Speech Recognition allows us to take what we hear and understand them.

Other Sensors

Radars, speedometers, sonars, oscilloscopes, weighing machines, etc. are all ways to determine a physical property of something, so they fall under the sensor category.

Reasoning

Reasoning is a process in which you use past information and relate it to the information that is provided to you at the moment. Below we will talk about some inference systems:

Natural Language Generation

This is a method with which humans determine and generate the language they will need to use in order to relay information to an object or another human in order to complete a task:

Logic-Based Inference

This process is used by human beings in order to determine if something is logically true.

Learning

Learning is a process in which a human develops new knowledge by using examples or training information. This functions similarly when it comes to machine learning.

Evidence-Based Inference

This inference allows the human to analyze evidence in order to draw a conclusion about whether a specific question should be answered with true or false.

Situation Assessment

This is the ability to realize what is going on around you on a more broad level.

Language Processing

Language processing can be described as the ability of humans to convert words that they heard into ideas and relations.

Planning/problem solving

The ability to detect something as a problem and find a solution for it.

Acting

After we receive information and consider it for long enough, we perform some sort of action. The following are all examples of acting.

Speech Generation

A person can vocalize a text given to them with great ease. They can read it and act accordingly due to speech generation.

Robotic Control

Another name for Robotic Control is muscular movement. It can be either willing or unwilling.

Examining the Components of AI

Aspects of machine reasoning and human cognition are both what researchers hope to achieve when it comes to AI. Most modern AI systems, including those that we mentioned before like Google's Assistant and Apple's Siri function by using the three layers.

The AI systems that function on three principles are a novelty. Still, they are the golden standard for now. They implement both speech recognition and generation, as well as language processing in order to understand what they are being asked to do so that they can execute a decision model. The model tells the AI which task it needs to perform. If, for example, the response is in the form of a speech component the system will get the signal to generate speech when the task is performed. These systems work efficiently as there is no pause between the transition from layer to layer. Let's talk about how sensing, reasoning, and acting, the three areas of intelligence functions in AI systems.

Sensing

We talked about two systems that work as speech recognition systems. Their function depends on the words that the user says. It recognizes what is being said based on waveforms of the words that are spoken. Different AI has different software that helps do this. Apple uses Nuance for Siri, while Google uses its own software. This is done through a microphone. There are systems that function based on other sensory effects as well.

You input the words via the microphone, but the AI doesn't understand the meaning of the words. AI interprets words is a similar way it would interpret text. They take the waveform and compares it to other waveforms until it gets a match. This means the machine is not aware of the word being a word, but a set of vibrations.

What it will output upon the finalization of this process is a series of words. The machine wants these words to make sense within the system. This will allow the system to interpret your command and provide you with the needed service. Language processing plays the most important part here.

Reasoning

There is a general pattern for analyzing a problem amongst intelligent systems, even though every system does it in its own way. In the previous example, systems could record you saying the name of some food. They will mark it and see if that food has a recipe. If it does not exist, but the user specifically asked for it, the program will assume that the speaker wants it to find a place where they can have pizza. Most other programs involved in AI of this type work similarly.

Lightweight processing is what we call this. It is based on the simplest of definitions and connections, which it can use to determine the difference between the command for finding a restaurant or a recipe. Another inference that the system can deduce is that the speaker would like to know where pizza can be found. The differentiation of how vs what needs to be done is the problem.

Every system is provided with the necessary information that is needed to satisfy needs. The information is received from the transition of sound to words. For example, if a system looked at the GPS and found restaurants that serve pizza and grade the options based on several parameters- price, rating, or proximity, in tandem with a user history, it would be able to provide you with a suitable location where you could enjoy a pizza. As you can see the system makes short work on comparing and grading parameters in order to provide the best possible answer.

Artificial intelligence accounts for the reasoning behind choosing one of the several different plans of action. These plans are usually scripts that are imported into the system in order to gather information. However one should not undermine their value solely on the fact that they are simple scripts. They are crucial to a system. Similar to how expertise works in humans, an AI is proficient in its job when it knows what needs to be done and when it needs to be done.

Acting

Results need to be given to the users upon the completion of sensing and reasoning within the AI system. What this usually ends up doing is it divides the ideas into several sets that can be returned to the user. They are then mapped into words and sentences which are then transformed into sound.

Assessing Data using AI

These systems always try to generalize human beings. Amazon, for example, takes what little information it has on you, such as what you buy and what sites you go to, and then compares this information to that of other people in order to predict your upcoming behavior. The data is what we call item transactional, meaning that it considers what you looked at and what you purchased as the same. Amazon uses this information as well in order to understand what products it should recommend.

Profile data makes up for only a small part of the process. Other information like customers, cluster objects, and others are taken into consideration on top of this data. The assumptions the algorithms are making about you can also be pulled out based on the place you live in and the amount of money you spend on average.

The results are always a set of characterizations:

- Based on what you have in common with somebody with similar interests in some of the categories, as well as what collections you like it could recommend some cookbooks.

- Based on things that you were looking at in a period of time, you could be someone who likes to take care of their garden.

- You just got yourself a well-decorated kitchen

The information on clusters, transactions and product categories are of great importance to retailers. When it comes to search engines, a history of information you looked for, what and where you clicked, as well as the items you viewed are all important things.

Predicting Outcomes with AI

One of the most important outcomes when it comes to reasoning are predictions. In order to prepare for what may happen in the potential future so you can deal with the outcomes more easily, predictions are important. AI has the same way of thinking.

Knowing what customers are going to buy is key for being a successful store manager. By looking at what products groups of customers bought or looked at and then projecting that pattern on other customers is how he achieves this. For example. You and your friend both like reading science fiction novels. If your friend likes to get new books fairly often, I can assume that you do too. Now if your friend appears multiple times in a sample of a few million people, you get the model which companies use to predict what people would buy.

Collaborative filtering is the combination of projecting a similarity and identifying it. It is what a lot of transactional recommendation systems use today. These systems base their assumptions on intuition in order to determine which people are similar to one another based on a certain parameter.

Classifying individuals and their behaviors into groups is another way you can use prediction. These groups would, of course, have to have some similarities in their profiles. Target applied the method while identifying pregnant women. This mapping was used in order to market products to these women more efficiently. This technique proved to be accurate. However, they were berated for this. Target found that certain women were not happy with the fact that their pregnancy was found about by family members this way.

It is difficult to separate features and actions from one another as they are linked very tightly. If you watched a movie franchise, it is safe to say that you watched one of the entries in that series. If you buy a baby crib, you are going to buy some blankets. If you opened a bank account, you will make some transactions soon. It's prediction like these that increase the need to categorize things and find similarities in individuals.

A prediction aims to find a problem that can possibly occur in the future and how it can be avoided or solved. The goal isn't finding the person who is receiving, but predict what they may go for.

Some systems use machine learning and data mining when they need to focus more on outcomes rather than make recommendations or predictions. These systems connect visible characteristics and features at a point in time with events that will need to be predicted in the future by looking at the frequency of the features when compared to the examples of what the system is predicting. This process of prediction gives rise to the following question, "What feature or behavior will predict this?"

Anything from buying something to a cyber-attack can be considered a "problem" in this context. With techniques like data mining, predictive analysis, and regression analysis, they aim to create rules that can predict the "problems" that may occur before they occur.

In the core of the systems that we interact with the most lie inferring, predicting and dynamic asserting and it's clear why. In order to predict what is going to happen in the future, we humans need to know what's going on now. It's similar to AI as it needs data to base its assumptions on. Making inferences about the event and predicting how it will develop is crucial as it helps anticipate what will happen in the future and helps us decide how to deal with it.

Chapter 9

Big Data

❋ ❋ ❋ ❋ ❋ ❋ ❋ ❋ ❋ ❋ ❋ ❋ ❋ ❋ ❋ ❋ ❋ ❋

2012 looked like the year in which big data technologies were the most prominent they would ever be. 2013 stole the crown, however, when big data analytics started popping up. Managing substantial amounts of data is going to be quite difficult, especially when you want to pull out the most important information from the bunch. Changing the way you think about working with data and the way you go about it will be forever changed by big data.

With larger datasets, it is quite difficult to apply the basic principles of data science. Trial and error is not always going to be a good method for finding solutions, especially when your dataset is large and heterogeneous. There are very few options that can process a large amount of data in a timely manner, so, with the increase of the size of the dataset, fewer and fewer options for making predictive models are available. Your analysis samples which are frozen in time, will also be limited due to the regular statistical solutions being more focused towards analytics that are static. This will have a chance of giving you results that are unreliable and surpassed.

Usually, data science is going to be trial and error, which is going to be impossible whenever working

Luckily there are some alternatives that will fix the issues that you may have with research domains which expand over time. One of which is, you guessed it, machine learning. Efforts are already being put into this. Different companies are making applications that focus on making algorithms that deliver you with accurate predictions. These applications are already used in statistics and pc sciences and are doing a good job so far.

Some applications will be able to tell businesses what products they should buy or if there is fraud detected. Giving a reliable analysis is going to be a breeze with machine learning. It uses generic and automatic methods which help simplify the scientist's task. It will also be able to figure out statistics themselves in real time.

Assessing, predicting and inferring are all used by most learning systems and artificial intelligence. These are all parts that play into human reasoning. They have a task of answering several fairly simple questions on a regular basis. "What is happening? What will happen next? What is going on around us?" are just some of the questions that it should answer.

We subconsciously assess, infer and predict whenever we are doing even the simplest of things. When we wait for a taxi, call an elevator or push a button on our device, we are doing all three. AI has recently started doing the same thing.

When it comes to Big Data a staggering 2.5 quintillion bytes of new data are accounted for every day. Here, possibly more than anywhere else, it is important to know how AI Systems work when it comes to capturing data, synthesizing it and driving their reasoning. Transforming numbers and unstructured data into something that humans can understand is a key thing that AI systems can do. This is especially important with problems like Big Data.

Understanding these systems is easy once you realize that the underlying processes are smart. They aim to make these processes understandable and simple, without damaging their intelligence. AI does not work on some sort of magic, but on the basis of algorithms fueled by data, power and scale.

What is Big Data?

There exist two very different sources of data which provide us with Big Data. Big Data is the collective name for all of the data that comes from these two sources. The first source accounts for all of the data found within an organization or a business. This data is shared amongst a huge network of users. It includes blogs, emails, PDFs, business events, process events, internal files, work documents, or any other structured, unstructured, and semi-structured data in general. The second source is the data that you may find outside of the organization. While this information is usually free as it is available to the general public, there is still some information in this field that you will need to pay to see. This information can be about products the competitors distribute, hints from third parties, information that pops up on social media, certain hierarchies, as well as complaints that were put up on regulatory sites by customers.

Big Data might look like data that was used in any period of time. However, Big Data is separated from other kinds of data based on the following four characteristics. The four Vs of Big Data are Volume. Variety, Velocity, and Veracity. These are the most prominent characteristics that make Big Data such a special phenomenon. Keep in mind, however, that there are several other characteristics, but none are as prominent as this.

Volume

Ever since Big Data caused turmoil in the world, many organizations started having problems with facilitating the vast flood of data in their data warehouses. Since the year 2006, several dozens of exabytes of data were made and this number just keeps on increasing more and more. This amount of data, thanks to Big Data, can now be collected in a matter of milliseconds, which means that a trillion gigabytes are collected every hour. Now that's an impressive number. What makes it even more impressive is that it does not show any signs of going forward.

Before Big Data organizations counted their collective data storage space in terabytes. Now they do the same in petabytes since the data has increased so exponentially. For some organizations in some industries, a strain on the analytics architecture can be noticed due to the volume of data they need to store. For example. Let's talk about some organizations in the communication industry. Let's say that the company has a hundred million customers. If the company was to collect daily data on all of the customers, it would take up more than 5 petabytes of space over a period of a hundred days. In the past, companies deleted their data daily, but recently regulators have been asking companies in the industry to keep records about calls or data usage of each customer

Velocity

Velocity is a difficult term to explain as it accounts for two phenomena. You can consider both the latency and throughput of data as part of this term. First, we will talk about latency. The infrastructure of analytics was a store - and - report kind of deal. Data from the previous day was made into reports and was represented as "D-1". Over the last several years it was deemed necessary to change how it works. It grew more and more difficult to cater to the needs of every business. An example of this would be an advertising agency that is looking to conduct analytics in order to place ads on platforms in milliseconds. This was not possible with the store - and - report module, as it was too slow to respond.

Now, the throughput of data. This is a second, but by no means less important, measure of velocity. It represents the flow of data through the analytics infrastructure. A rate of 80 percent was noticed when it comes to the rate at which global phone data is growing. It is speculated that the data collected annually will increase by 12-14 exabytes per year, as the sharing of different media has been made an easy thing to do. For a long time, corporations have been looking to create an infrastructure that will let them analyze the vast amounts of data in parallel.

Variety

Data Warehouse Technology was introduced in the late 90s of the last century. It's goal was to create and represent data through the usage of Meta-models aimed at simplifying data and helping to represent it in one form no matter the structure of the data. They mostly compiled data from multiple sources via ETL or ELT. The basic principle was narrowing the variety and ambiguity down so that the data could be properly applied and used. Big Data has expanded our views by allowing us to create new technologies for data integration. It also allowed for creative solutions in the infrastructure and analysis technologies. A great number of analytics are always on the look-out for solutions that would make aiding all of their customers in a timely manner a more easy task. This would also help in making a more clear connection between a disgruntled user and the operator, aiding the further solving of the problem. Call center data goes only as far as unstructured data like sound or text and rare bits of structured data. Many different applications gather different kinds of data from emails, documents, and blogs. Slice is one of the companies that provides analytic services for online orders. It uses raw data from many different sources and organizations. Some of the sources can be purchases, parking tickets, airline tickets, receipts and the like. Is there any way that this information could be compiled into product catalogs and be analyzed properly?

Veracity

Big Data comes from several sources outside of the companies control, while internal data is tightly governed. This is why Big Data can often come out false or inaccurate. This would usually slow down and reduce the quality of the analysis. Veracity, as a term, refers to the sustainability of the data. It also looks into how credible the sources are.

Let's try to define credibility in regards to sources of data. Organizations give the information on their products to third parties which provide that information to the customer care support or their contact center. Now, before the organization does that it needs to be assessed and credited as to not provide any false information. If the organization is proved to be trustworthy, the information can be used to help customers and assist them with their queries. Otherwise, the company might damage their own revenue by offering the customer with a wrong product or service. This could lead to different campaigns that boycott the company for its poor services. Social media would explode and damage the company's reputation. For example, a company could run a survey on products that it sells. If customers take a liking to the product, this information would be recorded and considered. On the other hand, if a customer states that they dislike the product and you don't incur as to why it is so, you are left with unstructured data that is of little use to you.

Chapter 10

Deep Neural Networks

❄ ❙ ❄ ❙ ❄ ❙ ❄ ❙ ❄ ❙ ❄ ❙ ❄ ❙ ❄ ❙ ❄ ❙ ❄ ❙ ❄ ❙ ❄ ❙ ❄ ❙ ❄

We can talk about neural network architecture now that you know more about deep learning and its applications. Neural networks are very important for machines. A properly programmed neural network will help the machine think like a person and process information in that way. These networks are made out of layers. These layers can process many kinds of information. Each layer is made out of neurons that all work together to solve problems. Since neural networks help machines think like humans, it makes sense that machines with neural networks are capable of learning. Pattern recognition and data classification are some of the things that these machines are used for.

When neurons change and adjust, the network can learn, similar to human beings.

A person who does not dabble with AI, somebody that you may talk to on the street, could be shocked to learn that they have encountered a lot of artificial intelligence and other kinds of machine learning. Millions of dollars are spent by some of the most popular companies in order to research that will improve their business. Some of these companies are Apple, Google, Facebook, Amazon, and IBM.

Our day to day lives might be impacted by this research already, even though you might not know it. With internet searches, for example, you will be shown options on websites and searches that match the keywords you typed in. Machine learning is important for this as it is the main thing that allows your browser to filter through the millions of possible recommendations.

The same principle is used in Netflix recommendations or spam filters that help filter through your emails. In the medical industry, this is used for the classification of medication and has an important role in the Human Genome Project where it goes through the countless combinations of patterns in DNA that can tell you something about your family history, risk factors, or health prospects.

These systems are applicable in most industries as they are highly adaptable and sophisticated. This is made possible through algorithms that guide the computer through many learning processes. With the correct algorithms, you can teach a system to detect abnormal behaviors that can happen within a pattern. This helps the system learn how to predict possible outcomes that may occur in a wide variety of situations.

An artificial neural network is something that contains algorithms of different kinds, data receptors and a plethora of other elements.

Ever since they were introduced during the 1950s, artificial neural networks have been a remedy when it comes to the future of science. They are patterned similarly to the human brain. They allow the machine to learn during the training phase of programming. This knowledge is then used as a foundation for solutions that would be applied to problems in the future.

Historical Background

Neural networks have been a thing since before computers. The problem was that people were not proficient enough for utilizing them. This is why the recent advances made in the field of neural networks are so important. Any developments in computer technologies help the research of neural networks. A craze started and people started being enthusiastic over the field. However, most attempts were fruitless, as no advancements that could help to improve the efficiency and accuracy of our machines. The enthusiasm started to decrease. However, some of the researchers remained steadfast and continued their studies. They worked hard in order to develop what we have now, a technology model that is accepted by most people in the industry.

The first artificial neural network was made by Warren McColloch and Walter Pitts in the year 1943. This was called the McCulloch-Pitts neurons. The network was not used to perform or automate complex tasks as the duo did not have the technology needed for the further development of the network.

What Are They and How Do They Work?

Terms like artificial intelligence, machine learning, and deep learning are all terms that refer to processes that are happening in and to the neural network. People might be skeptical when it comes to the way machines learn. However, we assure you that it really means that they are trained like human minds are.

A computational distributed model is made up of simple parallel processors with a plethora of tiny connections is a good way to think about these networks. The human brain is made from many, many neurons that are interconnected via synapses which allow them to make analysis and computations in our cerebral cortex. Learning is achieved with the change in the connections in our brains allow us to acquire new skills and learn new skills so that we can solve difficult problems.

A good way to think of these networks is to think of many simple parallel processors integrated with hundreds (or thousands) of tiny connections that make up a computational distributed model. In the human brain, there are millions of neurons all interconnected by synapses that allow them to make computations and analysis in the cerebral cortex. As these connections are made, learning is achieved allowing the person to acquire new skills so they can accomplish complex problems.

Hundreds of homogenous processing units that are interconnected through links are elements of a neural network. The unique configurations of connections and simplicity are what make this design truly beautiful. Data goes into the network through an input layer and goes to the output layer. In the meantime, the data is processed through the many layers in between until the problem is computed and a final solution is carried out.

Only a few units that transfer information were the gist of the structure of the simple neural networks in their earlier days. Today, however, a network could be made up of millions of different units that are intertwined and work together in order to emulate the process of learning. More modern networks are able to solve very difficult and complex problems in many ways.

Why use Neural Networks?

Large volumes of data are dedicated to making improvements to the industry by the industry itself. There are many variables in these datasets that can make it difficult for humans to find patterns in that appear in the datasets themselves. Via neural networks, we can recognize these patterns more easily. Without them, computers could find it to be a difficult task to identify trends in the dataset. By taking the time to train a neural network, an engineer can feed the network huge datasets in order to turn it into an expert in a selected area. With this trained network, the engineer can predict the output for any possible input. This also allows the engineer to be able to answer some questions about the future. Neural networks have many advantages and here are some of them:

- A neural network can adapt to new tasks and learn how to do new things because of it using supervised machine learning

- The network can be used to report back any information that was fed to it during the learning stage

- Machines with neural network architecture work far faster and provide more accurate results. This is because of the ability to compute data in parallel.

- Neural networks can be fixed fairly easily. While performance will be affected if the network is damaged, the network will still remember some of the properties.

The McCulloch-Pitts Neuron - What is It?

There are a lot of similarities between the human brain and artificial neural networks. This makes sense due to the fact that these networks were made to emulate how the human brain This much is easy to understand. The following are some of the similarities between them:

- Millions of artificial neurons make them up and each one of them can compute problems and solve them

- Each neuron has many different connections

- They are both non-linear and parallel

- They can learn through the change in the connection between units

- They adapt to new knowledge when they find an error instead of penalizing themselves

- Based on the data that they never came across before, they can produce outputs

These all describe how the neural network, as a whole, works. While the two are very similar on the surface, we should look into how the smallest of the units work. The McCulloch-Pitts neuron is the smallest part of the network.

In the brain, the basic unit of processing is a neuron. In the artificial neural network, this unit is the main part of processing any type of information and calculations of any kind. It is made from the following three elements:

- The weight and synaptic efficacy of connections, as well as the connections themselves

- An agent that summarizes and processes input signals and outputs linear combinations

- A system that limits the neuron's output

The 1940s was the first time that the MCP neuron was introduced. This neuron got its name from the logician Walter Pitts and the neuroscientist Warren S. McCulloch. They tried to understand what happens inside of the human brain when we try to produce and understand complex patterns and replicate them through the connections between the many basic cells.

The design of old systems was very simple. The input was quantified from zero to one and the output was limited to the same domain. Every input was either inhibitory or excitatory. This simplicity made the design limited the learning capabilities of the machine.

While sometimes simplicity can be great, it also has its downfalls. It costs the computational ability to comprehend complex topics.

The MCP neuron was supposed to sum up all of the inputs. The neuron takes all of the positives and negatives that appear and compiles them, adding plus one if an input is positive and taking one away if the input is negative.

Neural Networks versus Conventional Computers

Neural networks and computers do not apply the same kind of solution to every problem. The latter usually use algorithms in order to find solutions. Conventional computers also have another method of solving a problem. If you taught it the steps that it should follow it should do good by them in order to find a solution. What this tells us is that humans and computers can solve similar problems. Where computers shine is solving problems that people can't.

As we have said numerous times, the human brain and neural networks work in a similar manner: through a network of interconnected neurons. These networks usually work in parallel for the best efficiency. An engineer can teach a network to complete a task by giving it an example of how it should approach the solution. This means that selecting the data you feed to the system is very important. If you are not careful when selecting the data you might make it harder for the system to learn the process. The networks are unpredictable as, due to the data they are fed, it might learn to solve problems that the engineer didn't foresee.

Computers apply some cognitive approaches when solving problems, as well. If the engineer gives the computer proper instructions the computer can act on them and solve problems. Using a high-level programming language, it takes only a few steps for the engineer to provide the instructions to the computer. The computer, later, takes these instructions and translates it into a language that the computer can understand. This process allows the engineer to predict how the computer will go about solving certain problems. If the computer reports a problem while processing, the engineer can conclude that there should be an error in the software or hardware.

Conventional computers work in tandem with neural networks. Arithmetic calculations are a kind of task that is best solved by conventional algorithmic computers. On the other hand, other, more complex tasks, can be solved by neural networks most efficiently. Most tasks are best solved by combining the two approaches so that the machine can work at peak efficiency,

Types of Neural Networks

Fully connected neural network

A network layer is the most basic type of neural network architecture. It is composed out of three layers of neurons which are interconnected. The input layer is the first layer. It is connected to a hidden layer of neurons which then proceed to the output layer. The input layer is where the engineer gives data to the system. The nodes that connect the hidden layer and the input layer dictate how the input layer views the data it is given. What kind of data outputted depends on the weights and connections between the secret layer and output layer.

This kind of architecture is simple, but still interesting because the hidden layers can represent data in many ways. The weights mentioned before are nodes that connect layers. They also determine when these layers need to be activated. An engineer can modify these weights and change the way the layers interact. He can do this to ensure the way the hidden layer shows data is conducted the correct way.

It is fairly easy to tell a multilayer and single-layer architecture apart. When it comes to single-layer architecture, neurons are connected at the nodes. This means that the processing power of the network is maximized due to all of the layer being interconnected. When it comes to multilayer architecture there are more layers to the system. Here neurons are not interconnected, but the layers are.

Perceptrons

The term perception was coined in 1960 by Frank Rosenblatt. This happened during a time where neural network architecture developed greatly. Perceptions represent a kind of McCulloch and Pitts model which is assigned a pre-processing and fixed weight. This makes the system easier to use when it comes to recognizing the patterns, resembling the function in human beings. This network can be used in other processes too.

Feed-forward Networks

There are several names for this kind of network. Bottom-up or top-down are both alternative names for feed-forward networks. This means that signals and data will flow in only one direction, from the input point to the output point. This network does not have a feedback loop. This means that output gotten in one instance will not affect output that comes in another layer. This is one of the simplest networks to make as input is directly associated with output. This network is often used in recognizing patterns.

Convolutional neural networks

Fully connected neural networks are what convolutional neural networks bears the most similarity to. Many layers made from many neurons are what makes up this system. Each neuron is assigned with a weight. This is due to the training data that was used during the teaching phase. When input is given to a neuron they will make a dot product, which is followed by a non-linearity. You might wonder what the difference between a fully connected neural network and a convolutional network is. A CNN views each input in the original dataset to be an image which an engineer can encode properties of the system into. This reduces the number of instances in the original dataset and it makes it easier for the network to use the forward function. These types of neural networks are used by most deep learning programs.

Feedback networks

Feedback networks are specific due to the movement of the signals. They flow in both directions and induce a loop into the network.

These networks are extremely difficult to make, but are very powerful. The network will function in a state of absolute equilibrium until you create a change. This state of constant change will continue until the system equalizes again. If an engineer feeds a new dataset to the system, it will try to find a new point of equilibrium. This is the reason why feedback networks are recurrent and interactive. Below we will discuss recurrent neural networks.

Recurrent neural networks

Recurrent neural networks are special because the information always loops. The network will consider the input and asses what it has learned, once it decides. RNN usually has short-term memory. In combination with Long Short-term memory, it gains long-term memory. We will further discuss this bellow.

It is difficult to explain RNN without using an example. Let's say that the network you are using is a regular feed-forward neural network. Let's say that you input the word "brain". The system will separate the word into characters and go over them one by one, always forgetting the previous characters. This means that this model cannot be used to predict which character is next unless it has already been gone over. Due to its internal memory, an RNN remembers previous characters and predicts the next ones. While producing outputs, it copies them and puts them back into the network itself. This means that RNNs will produce, on top of the present information, five immediate past information. Due to all of this, the following inputs are all a part of an RNN:

- The Present Data

- The Recent Data

As always, the dataset selection is very important. The dataset used to teach the model will affect how the system uses sequences while predicting upcoming characters in a text. This places RNN in front of most algorithms when it comes to the functions they can perform. Unlike a feed-forward network, RNN applies weight to both the previous and current input data and shifts the weights that have already been assigned, while a feed-forward network assigns weights to neurons in each layer in order to produce and output.

Generative adversarial network

A GAN, also known as a generative adversarial network, is made up of two networks that have been pitted against each other. Due to this, we call it an adversarial network. GAN can be used by most engineers in a system, because it can learn to mimic any distribution or dataset. GAN can be used to build something that is unique to you in many domains. It can simultaneously process pictures, prose, speech, etc. You are bound to be impressed by the output of these networks.

A generator and a discriminator are parts of this network. The discriminator evaluates instances made by the generator, while the generator creates the data instances themselves. The discriminator's job is to identify if a new instance is from a premade training dataset or not.

Training the Neural network

Training your neural network is one of the most important parts of making a neural network. There are a few methods to do this, however, only one method has the most positive results. Error backpropagation, also known as the error propagation algorithm, symmetrically adjusts the weights on connections and neurons. This means that if the system makes a mistake it will learn from it and come closer to the correct solution every time.

This kind of training has two stages: stage 1, also known as the forward propagation, and stage 2, also known as back propagation.

In stage 1, a calculation of all of the activated neurons in all of the layers is performed. During this stage, there is no change to synaptic connection weights. What this means is that the default values will be used in the first iteration of the system. During phase 2, however, we are given an actual answer from the network and we can compare the output to the expected output in order to determine the error rate.

The error rate is then taken into account and it is returned to one of the synaptic connections. Modifying the weights then decreases the difference between the expected value and the value we got. This process happens on and on until the error margin is decreased to the point where it can't be decreased anymore.

- Forward Propagation: in forward propagation, the first input is the initial data that is then transferred to the hidden layers where it is processed until an output is produced. The activation functions, the depth of the data, and the width of the data all depend on the basic architecture of the network. Depth tells us how many hidden layers exist within the system. The width tells us the number of neurons in each layer and the activation functions instruct the system on exactly what to do.

- Backward Propagation: It allows for the weight of the connections to be adjusted via a supervised learning algorithm. This is done in order to reduce the difference between the solution we got and the expected solution.

Neural networks are a very interesting field of study and keeps getting more and more intricate, now using machine learning. It has a huge amount of potential to aid the creation of future developments in computer science.

- They are adept at solving problems whose solutions require a certain degree of error

- They can use experience from solving previous problems and use it to solve problems it encounters for the first time.

- Their implementation is a piece of cake as the definitions for duplication, neurons, and creating connections are easy to understand

- It completes operations fairly quickly as every neuron operates on only the value it received as input

- Stable outputs directly relate to the input values

- Before producing a result, they can take all of the inputs into accounts

Neural networks still have a few drawbacks, even with all of those advantages. Some of them are:

- It has a certain similarity to black boxes. You can determine what happened, but there is no way to determine why a certain result was produced

- The memory cannot be described or localized in the network itself

- They can only be used by computers with compatible hardware as they have unique computer needs

- Producing proper calculations can be very time consuming, however, as the training techniques are extensive and can take a while to execute.

- The only method of solving problems is algorithms and you have to give them the correct one for the problem

- The accuracy of the output values can vary

- A large number of examples is needed for a good learning process that can produce solutions to be made

Neural networks are completely capable of independent decision making based on the number of inputs and variables. Because of this, they can create an unlimited number of recurring iterations to solve problems without human interference. When we see these networks in action, you'll find a numeric vector that represents the various types of input data. These vectors could be anything from pixels, audio and/or video signals, or just plain words. These vectors can be adjusted via a series of functions producing an output result.

At first glance, you might think that there is not that much to say about neural networks. However, when you look into it a bit more, you start to see the intricacies behind it. The same system can be used to handle the most basic of problems and the most complex alike. The only thing that changes is the number of weights that are placed on each value.

Conclusion

❉ ı ❉ ı ❉ ı ❉ ı ❉ ı ❉ ı ❉ ı ❉ ı ❉ ı ❉ ı ❉ ı ❉ ı ❉ ı ❉ ı ❉

You've made it! If you're finished with this book, you should be proud of yourself. You've made it through some seriously difficult math, programming, and theory.

If you're wondering about what next steps you should take, I recommend using online tutorials. After all, there's only so much content a book can cover, and the field of ML is forever evolving.

Other than that, start your own project! Simply studying can't teach you as much as your own project would. Try to make a funny script generator. You could analyze lines from movies and have the computer compile them.

There are countless things you can do with ML-that is why it's so popular after all.

It is clear to see how far computer science has come. However, it is important to remember that this is not something that happened in the past decade or so. The roots of every great "discovery" of the past 20 years lie in the 50' and 60' of the past century. The principles of computer science always stayed the same, it is just our methods that have changed and our technology that has advanced. When the first neural network was created, it is hard to believe that they could imagine how far they could, or, for that matter, would evolve.

We are living in a huge crossroads of technology where we are having new break-throughs constantly. It is easy to assume that, soon enough, we will be able to do things that we cannot even comprehend right now. The neural networks themselves were revived solely because of the advancement we made in 50 years and since our technology is growing more and more rapidly. It is not a stretch to say that we might have a breakthrough just as big in 10 or so years. The best part about it is that understanding such complex things is becoming an easier task, more and more so as time passes by.

Complex things like Artificial Intelligence and Machine Learning are becoming easier and easier to understand. AI is becoming a part of our lives even today and has some excellent uses, not only in your household but in many fields of science as well. In medicine, AI is used to sort out data and, in some parts of the world, distribute medication based on prescriptions. AI like Siri is not something that few people know about. It is relatively advanced and serves its purpose quite well, especially considering the limitations of such a software.

These AI have many flaws and many things that need to be improved. We just do not have the technology we need to make our concepts a reality. But just imagine it. A world where Siri can recognize the meaning behind your words and make an approximation of what you meant to say through your phrases and slang. Now imagine an AI that is tailored to your needs. An AI that understands you and keeps track of your needs and requests. An AI that adapts to you and learns from you.

This might sound like something from a science fiction movie, but it is an actual possibility. Computer science has already gotten so far that we are almost able to perfectly emulate the thought process a human goes through when performing several actions. When broken down into smaller processes and components, this can seem quite simple, but what you need to understand is that this is no small thing. Countless hours of research and work was put into it in order to make it work. Decades of experience in the field stands tall behind this. Brilliant minds from all across the world and different periods of time poured all of their brilliance into the ideas that will become the very principle this works on.

The insane amount of data we accumulate every year speaks volumes about how far we have gotten. Just the unit of data we measure our yearly influx in seemed unobtainable not so long ago. Big Data had a massive impact on the world. It revolutionized, not only the data market, but how we approach data as well. The amounts of data we receive, as well as how much we need to improve is dictated by Big Data. We need to keep up. This makes Big Data a point in the right direction. It pushes us to improve and surpass our old limits.

What people need to understand is that the field of computer science is almost like a living organism. When one area goes through a breakthrough, all of the others follow to even out. It works in such synergy where advancements in certain areas lead to advances in other areas. This complex system of upgrading upon the previous knowledge of those who surround you is the basis of any kind of progress. There is also competition for those who will get the most out of their resources and skills. Another thing to take note of about the discoveries made recently is that they are not a product of a company's adventurous spirit.

Most of the progress comes out of one of two things. One- a company comes to an incredible advancement due to a company wanting to outclass its competitors in something so they pour enough money and research into it. Eventually, this work bears fruit and we have ourselves a foundation for something new. The second option is that somebody conceptualizes an idea and, if we have the technology for it, uses the idea to create something completely new which, again, functions as a foundation for another field of study. Even a laboratory is a place of business, quite a volatile one for that matter. Not only does it pit corporation versus corporation, but individual versus individual as well. Progress comes from the need to be the first at something or better at something else.

People always debate about what the most prominent advancement in computer sciences is. I would say that, without a doubt, it is machine learning. Now let me explain why. Machine learning has gotten us several steps closer to the ultimate goal which is making a machine that can perfectly emulate the way people think and work. This might seem a bit far-fetched but it is a serious possibility. As I stated before, we already have systems that can emulate human behavior with tasks like noticing patterns. Where this differs from actual human behavior is that the machine needs to be told exactly what it needs to do to solve that problem.

Machine learning takes it a step higher and allows the machine to gain new techniques and algorithms by learning. This is a difficult process where you need to feed your machine with a ton of data over a long period of time, as well as show it how to solve a problem. The machine will eventually learn how to solve the problem, as well as any problem that functions on a similar principle. However, if you stimulate and feed the machine for long enough, eventually it will learn how to teach itself. Now, this is the interesting part. The machine itself will start perceiving the lack of a solution to a problem, a problem of its own. This will make the machine find a solution to the problem of not having the solution to another problem. This way the machine learns how to deal with problems on its own. You might be thinking: " Well if machines can do all of those things, what makes their processing different from how humans think?". Well, there are two answers to this question. The first is that the machine simply does not understand what it is doing. It recognizes the pattern of motions it needs to take in order to solve a problem, but does not connect any of those steps to anything outside the problem. This means that the term "brain" is registered by a line of 1s and 0s and, to the machine's understanding, the same line of 1s and 0s will always mean "brain".

This is where the machine is successful in emulating a human, as it connects a term to a signal, which is stored in the core of the machine. Where the machine fails it the fact that it cannot perceive the word "brain" as anything other than that same line of 1s and 0s. The other difference is that the machine cannot take data on its own. Every machine needs to be fed data before it could start doing anything. While the same is true for humans, humans can take data from their surroundings. A machine that had no data fed to it is similar to a new-born in that is the most basic form and the first step in the evolution of its species. A machine that has nobody to feed it data is a machine that cannot learn.

On the other hand, a child will be able to determine if it is cold, hot or in pain due to the chemical reactions happening in the child's body. Though the child has no understanding of the meaning of the word pain, the chemical reaction makes it clear that something is wrong here and the child will be inclined not to repeat the course of action ever again as it will not want to experience the same sensation. The computer, however, cannot gather data before having a certain amount of data. Let's be generous and say that the computer starts off with a way to gather data from its surroundings and process it. Here it differs from humans in two ways, yet again. If the computer encounters a problem, it can have all the data in the world, but it will remain stuck on that problem, as there is no one to tell it if the solution it made is correct or not, while a child will have an automatic aversion to pain and will know that staying away from it is the best course of action without any instructions.

The other problem is that, without the help of a human, a machine could not tie data to problems. You can load as much data as you would like, if it does not have something to use that data for, the computer does not really have a purpose. Here we have the main thing about the difference between machines and humans. Humans are born with a certain set of instinctual reactions, while a machine has none. If a machine would encounter a problem, and the problem is not registered as a problem within the machine, the machine will do absolutely nothing. While, yes, some machines can do things that people cannot do and compute massive amounts of data that we could never hope to, they still greatly rely on humans for a sense of direction. They are, by all means, lost without us.

There are people who believe that if we continue progressing like this, a time will come when we are all slaves to machines and that machines will replace us all, but this is highly unlikely. While they are impressive creations, machines require humans to work. Without humans, machines are meaningless and have no objective value. One could speculate on what the machines themselves could do to improve themselves, but we will not talk about this as it is more in the realm of science fiction.

Now, look at literally every machine in the world. All of them have had programmers, and have been programmed for a certain purpose. "But what about computers?", you might ask. Well, even though computers were programed to do various things...your computer can't do things on its own; in the end you can always simply pull its plug.

The fear of a robot uprising is innately tied to science fiction, because there is no reason for anyone to make such a thing. There lies no profit in making a lifelike robot. After all, the main reason for making machine learning algorithms is capitalism. If there is no profit in it, then it won't prosper in today's capitalistic society.

To conclude, while computer science has had quite a boom lately, this did not happen out of nowhere. This is a process that started long ago and who knows when it will stop, but one thing is for certain. The ability of humans to destroy can only be surpassed by their ability to create. While it might seem that we have reached the pinnacle in certain areas, we might just be scratching the surface. One can only speculate how far machines will get if machine learning continues to grow at this rate and even then, one's speculations could fall flat, as there is no telling what a brilliant mind of a random stranger or machine could come up with next. Maybe there will come a time where machines can learn from one another.

Fundamentally, I hope that this book has taught you something new about machine learning. Even if you skipped the mathematical portions, I hope you found the rest of the book comprehensible and interesting. The subject of machine learning is vast, so naturally there are some topics that haven't been covered.

The main topics have been exhaustively covered and detailed both mathematically and in theory. Hopefully this has helped you deepen your understanding of machine learning. Finally, I hope you continue on this path, and one day I can look up to you to teach me, instead of vice-versa.

References

Liu, Y. (2017). *Python machine learning by example: Easy-to-follow examples that get you up and running with machine learning*. Birmingham: Packet.

Marsland, S. (2015). *Machine learning: An algorithmic perspective*. Boca Raton: CRC Press.

Your First Machine Learning Project in Python Step-By-Step. (n.d.). Retrieved from https://machinelearningmastery.com/machine-learning-in-python-step-by-step/

CPSIA information can be obtained
at www.ICGtesting.com
Printed in the USA
LVHW061119170723
752637LV00002B/325